The Genealogist's
Census Pocket Reference

THE
GENEALOGIST'S
Census
Pocket
Reference

Tips, Tricks & Fast Facts
to Track Your Ancestors

From Allison Dolan and the Editors of *Family Tree Magazine*

**FAMILY
TREE
BOOKS**

Cincinnati, Ohio
shopfamilytree.com

PUBLISHER/
EDITORIAL
DIRECTOR
Allison Dolan

EDITED BY
**Jacqueline
Musser**

DESIGNED BY
Christy Miller

PRODUCTION
COORDINATED BY
Mark Griffin

For more genealogy resources, visit
<shopfamilytree.com>.

16 15 14 13 12   5 4 3 2 1

ISBN: 978-1-4403-2145-0

Distributed in Canada by Fraser Direct
100 Armstrong Ave.
Georgetown, Ontario, Canada L7G 5S4
Tel: (905) 877-4411

**Distributed in the U.K. and Europe
by F&W Media International, LTD**
Brunel House, Forde Close, Newton Abbot,
TQ12 4PU, UK
Tel: (+44) 1626 323200
Fax: (+44) 1626 323319
E-mail: enquiries@fwmedia.com

Distributed in Australia by Capricorn Link
P.O. Box 704, Windsor, NSW 2756 Australia
Tel: (02) 4577-3555

TABLE OF Contents

9 INTRODUCTION

10 HOW TO USE THIS BOOK

11 CHAPTER 1: CENSUS FACTS
    12 Official Census Dates
    12 Census Timeline
    15 Lost or Missing Censuses
    17 The Soundex Key
    19 The Lost Rule of Soundex
    19 Soundex Index
    20 US Census Record Websites
    21 Census Search Do's and Don'ts
    22 Online Census Search Tips
    23 Enumeration Districts
    24 Finding Addresses
    25 Famous Names in Censuses

27 CHAPTER 2: CENSUS MAPS
Areas Enumerated in Each Census from 1790 to 1940

59 CHAPTER 3: CENSUS QUESTIONS
Questions on Each Census from 1790 to 1940
    80 Census Questions by Category
    82 1920 and 1930 Censuses: Foreign Languages

87 CHAPTER 4: ENUMERATOR INSTRUCTIONS
Specific Instructions to Ennumerators for Each Census from 1790 to 1940

101 CHAPTER 5: CENSUS ABBREVIATIONS
  102 Relationships
  103 Citizenship Status
  103 Color/Ethnicity
  103 Employment
  103 Occupations
  104 Ownership of Home
  104 Military
  105 War
  105 Deaf, Dumb, Blind, Idiotic
  105 Other Abbreviations
  105 Names

107 CHAPTER 6: CENSUS RESULTS
  108 Historical US Population
  109 Most Common Ancestries in the 2000 US Census
  110 Foreign-Born Population Chart

121 CHAPTER 7: STATE AND
TERRITORY CENUSES
Dates of Colonial, Territorial and State Censuses for all 50 States
plus District of Columbia, America Samoa, Cuba, Guam, Panama
Canal Zone, Philippines, Puerto Rico and US Virgin Islands

135 CHAPTER 8: SPECIAL SCHEDULES
  136 Schedule of Defective, Dependent and Delinquent
  Classes
  145 Agricultural Censuses
  146 Slave Schedules
  146 Mortality Schedules
  147 Veterans and Military Censuses
  149 American Indian Censuses

151 CHAPTER 9: INTERNATIONAL CENSUSES

    152 Canada
    153 Czech Republic
    154 Denmark
    154 England and Wales
    155 Finland
    156 France
    157 Gemany
    157 Greece
    158 Hungary
    158 Italy
    159 Ireland
    160 Mexico
    161 Netherlands
    161 Norway
    162 Romania
    163 Russia
    163 Scotland
    164 Spain
    165 Sweden
    165 Google Translate

167 CHAPTER 10: CENSUS RESOURCES

    168 Books
    169 Websites: Research Helps and Portals
    174 Websites: State Indexes and Images
    176 Canadian and UK Records
    178 Organizations

179 CHAPTER 11: RESEARCH TRACKER

Introduction

Genealogists have a love-hate relationship with the US census. Yes, we love the reams of data those every 10-years population tabulations created, but we loathe inscrutably handwritten enumeration sheets. Between census appearances, ancestors often seem to switch not just residences but birth dates, too. Names can be indecipherable or all too common (is that your James Smith or somebody else's?). Offspring mysteriously appear and disappear. Worst, in some head counts, your ancestors simply refuse to be found at all.

To help you best utilize the census, we've gathered key resource lists, definitions, dates and other reference information from *Family Tree Magazine* and FamilyTreeMagazine.com <familytreemagazine.com> and put it all into this guide. Stash it in your bag, your desk or even your pocket, and pull it out whenever you need some insight on your enumeration examination.

How to Use This Book

Check the table of contents of this book to familiarize yourself with the information inside it. When you come across a census word or acronym you don't know, want to try a new website, have to calculate a Soundex code, want to learn how common your national heritage is, or need other pertinent information, look at the table of contents of this book, turn to the appropriate chapter and go to the section you need. Whenever your research uncovers a new resource or information that's pertinent to your family history, write it down in chapter 10, designed especially for you to record your favorite reference material.

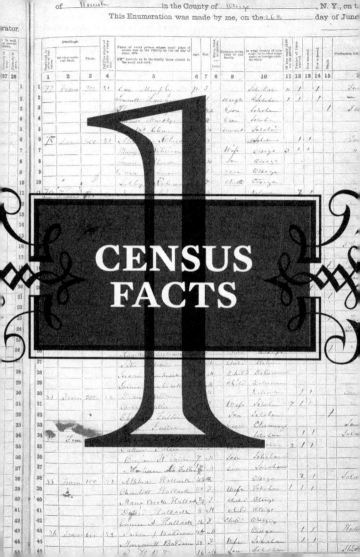

OFFICIAL CENSUS DATES

Congress designated an offical date for each census. The census was to record the population exactly as it was on the official census date. However, enumerators may have visited an address days or weeks after the offical census date. Although enumerators were instructed not to record anyone born after the official census date, families were sometimes confused and reported the birth anyway. The same is true for deaths. If a person died after the census date but before the enumerator visited, the person was to be counted for that census, but again, because of confusion the dead were sometimes not counted.

1790: August 2
1800: August 4
1810: August 6
1820: August 7
1830–1880: June 1
1890: June 2
1900: June 1
1910: April 15
1920: January 1
1930: October 1, 1929 (Alaska only)
1930–2010: April 1

CENSUS TIMELINE

1787 The Constitution is ratified, requiring a decennial population count to apportion representatives in Congress.

1790 Federal marshals count 3.9 million people in the first census by going door-to-door through the 13 states plus the districts of Maine, Vermont, Kentucky and the Southwest Territory.

1820 Respondents are asked if engaging in agriculture, commerce or manufacturing.

1830 The first printed questionnaires are used for collecting census data.

1840 Questions on agriculture, mining and fishing are added to the census.

1850 All free persons are recorded by name, along with their occupation and place of birth.

1861 Census data is used during the Civil War to measure relative military strengths and manufacturing abilities of the Union and Confederacy.

1868 The 14th Amendment ends the three-fifths counting rule for African-Americans.

1870 American Indians are first enumerated, excluding those living on reservations.

1880 Congress establishes a census office in the Department of the Interior.

1890 The 1890 census is the first to use punchcards and an electrical tabulation system.

1900 The Departments of War and the Navy enumerate military personnel, including those who were abroad.

1902 Congress authorizes a permanent census office, which is transferred the following year to the Department of Commerce and Labor.

1913 The Department of Commerce splits with the Department of Labor, bringing with it the US Census Bureau.

1919 Congress allows individuals to request copies of the census for genealogical purposes.

1921 The 1890 returns are destroyed by an unexplained fire.

1930 Following the onset of the Great Depression, the Census Bureau begins asking questions about unemployment and income.

1940 The Census Bureau creates an additional long form to be answered by a small percentage of the population.

1950 UNIVAC I, a computer, is used to help tabulate results.

1960 Questionnaires are mailed to urban households to be completed and mailed back to the Census Bureau.

1970 For the first time, respondents are asked to check off whether they are of Spanish or Hispanic origin or descent.

1990 The 1990 census is the first to be less accurate than the count preceding it, with an estimated 8.4 million people missed and another 4.4 million counted twice.

1999 The Supreme Court rules statistical samplings cannot be used to apportion congressional seats.

2000 For the first time, the Census Bureau runs a nationwide advertising campaign to encourage people to fill out their forms.

2010 The long form is replaced by the Census Bureau's annual American Community Survey.

LOST OR MISSING CENSUSES

All censuses miss some individuals here or there, but in some cases, records have been lost for various censuses and counties or cities. The largest record lost occurred in 1921 when a fire in the Commerce Department damaged or destroyed the 1890 census. Only 1 percent of the 1890 census documents survived the fire.

Missing census records by state:

ALABAMA 1820; territorial records available for Baldwin, Conecuh, Dallas, Franklin, Limestone, St. Clair, Shelby and Wilcox counties in the Alabama Historical Quarterly, vol. 6 (Fall 1944)

ALASKA 1870, 1880

ARKANSAS 1820

CALIFORNIA 1850 (Contra Costa, San Francisco and Santa Clara counties only)

DELAWARE 1790

DISTRICT OF COLUMBIA 1810

FLORIDA 1860 (Hernando County only)

GEORGIA 1790, 1800 (except Oglethorpe County), 1810, 1820 (Franklin, Rabun and Twiggs counties only)

ILLINOIS 1810

INDIANA 1800, 1810, 1820 (Daviess County only), 1830 (Wabash County only)

KENTUCKY 1790, 1800

LOUISIANA 1860 (Bienville County only)

MAINE 1800 (part of York County only), 1810 (half of Oxford County), 1820 (Houlton Plantation in Washington County only)

MARYLAND 1790 (Allegheny, Calvert, Somerset and part of Dorchester counties only), 1800 (Baltimore County outside of city of Baltimore only), 1830 (Montgomery, Prince George's, Queen Anne's, St. Mary's and Somerset counties only)

MASSACHUSETTS 1800 (Boston and part of Suffolk County only), 1890 veterans (Worcester County only)

MICHIGAN 1810

MISSISSIPPI 1830 (Pike County only), 1860 (Hancock, Sunflower and Washington counties only)

MISSOURI 1810, 1820

NEW HAMPSHIRE 1800 (part of Rockingham and Strafford counties only), 1820 (Grafton County and parts of Rockingham and Strafford counties only)

NEW JERSEY 1790 through 1820 (except 1800 Cumberland County)

NEW YORK 1810 (Cortland and part of Broome counties only)

NORTH CAROLINA 1790 (Caswell, Granville and Orange counties only), 1810 (Craven, Greene, New Hanover and Wake counties only)

OHIO 1800 and 1810 (except Washington County), 1820 (Franklin and Wood counties only)

PENNSYLVANIA 1800 (part of Westmoreland County only), 1810 (parts of Bedford, Cumerland and Philadelphia counties only), 1820 (parts of Lancaster and Luzerne counties only), 1870 (Philadelphia City, ward 27 only)

SOUTH CAROLINA 1800 (Richland District only), 1820 through 1850 (Clarendon County only)

TENNESSEE 1790, 1800, 1810 (except Grainger and Rutherford counties), 1820 (Anderson, Bledsoe, Blount, Campbell, Carter, Claiborne, Cocke, Grainger, Greene, Hamilton, Hawkins, Jefferson, Knox, McMinn, Marion, Monroe, Morgan, Rhea, Roane, Servier, Sullivan and Washington counties only)

TEXAS 1860 (Tarrant County only)

VIRGINIA 1790, 1800 (except Accomack and Louisa counties), 1810 (Alexandria, Cabell, Grayson, Greenbrier, Halifax, Hardy, Henry, James City, King William, Lee, Louisa, Mecklenburg, Middlesex, Nansemond, Northampton, Orange, Patrick, Pittsylvania, Russell and Tazwell counties only)

WASHINGTON 1860 (Benton, Columbia, San Juan, Snohomish and Stevens counties only), 1870 (Benton and Columbia counties only)

THE SOUNDEX KEY

The 1880, 1900 and 1920 federal censuses, plus parts of the 1910 and 1930 censuses, are indexed by state using a code based on the sounds in your ancestors' surnames. This indexing system—called Soundex—is especially useful when you don't know specifically where the family was living in the census year. The family's Soundex card will tell you their county and community, and where you can find their names on the census. Soundex most often is available as microfilm of the cards on which basic census information was written. Names with the

SOUNDEX CODE	LETTERS
1	b f p v
2	c g j k q s x z
3	d t
4	l
5	m n
6	r
no code	a e h i o u w y

same code appear together in the Soundex. (Note that the 1880 Soundex includes only households with children ages 10 and under.)

The Soundex indexing system uses a four-character code to help you find similar-sounding surnames in US census records. The code for a surname consists of the first letter of the name plus three numbers representing consonants. Use the following steps to code your ancestors' names.

1. Write the surname. Excepting the first letter, cross out any vowels and the letters *h*, *y* and *w*.

2. Use the first letter of the name as the first letter of your four-character code.

3. Match each subsequent consonant with the corresponding code from the key above until you have three numbers. Ignore the rest of the letters. If adjacent letters have the same number, ignore the second letter. If you run out of letters before your code has three numbers, complete the code with zeros.

DOBUSH: D120 (coding D-b-s)

GUTIERREZ: G362 (coding G-t-r-z)

LEE: L000 (coding the L)

PFISTER: P236 (coding P-s-t-r)

WASHINGTON: W252 (coding W-s-n-g)

THE LOST RULE OF SOUNDEX

A Soundex code determined using the "lost rule" (also known as the H and W Rule) may yield better search results for surnames having an *h* or *w* between two letters of the same code number. Such instances exist in names with combinations such as *thd* or *tht* (such as Rothdeutsch and Smithton), *chs* (Sachse, Ochs), *chk* (Wichkoski) and *schk* (Mitschke, Peschke).

When you formulate a Soundex code in such cases, disregard the *h* or *w* and push the like-coded letters together. For example, *chs* or *schk* would be coded as a single 2, not 22. These examples show the use of the lost rule:

ASHCROFT: A261 (coding A-sc-r-f)

MITSCHKE: M320 (coding M-t-sck-0)

ROTHDEUTSCH: R332 (coding R-td-t-sc)

SCHSEKOWESKE: S220 (coding Scs-k-sk-0)

SOCHSE OR SACHSE: S200 (coding S-cs-0-0)

SMITHTON: S535 (coding S-m-tt-n)

SOUNDEX INDEX

These census records have Soundex indexes:

1880 households with children ages 10 and under

1900 all states

1910 Alabama, Arkansas, California, Florida, Georgia, Illinois, Kansas, Kentucky, Louisiana, Michigan, Mississippi, Missouri, North Carolina, Ohio, Oklahoma, Pennsylvania,

South Carolina, Tennessee, Texas, Virginia and West Virginia

1920 all states

1930 all of Alabama, Arkansas, Florida, Georgia, Louisiana, Mississippi, North Carolina, South Carolina, Tennessee and Virginia; these Kentucky counties: Bell, Floyd, Harlan, Kenton, Muhlenberg, Perry and Pike; these West Virginia counties: Fayette, Harrison, Kanawha, Logan, McDowell, Mercer and Raleigh

US CENSUS RECORD WEBSITES

$ = subscription required to access most records

$ ANCESTRY.COM <ancestry.com>: all extant population census records and every-name indexes

ANCESTRY LIBRARY EDITION: all extant population census records and every-name indexes (available at subscribing libraries)

$ ARCHIVES.COM <archives.com>: all extant population census records, every-name indexes and images of all original records

FAMILYSEARCH <www.familysearch.org>: every-name index and transcription for 1850–1880 and 1900–1930; 1850 mortality schedule and slave schedule; 1890 census of Union veterans and widows of the Civil War; 1930 Census of merchant seaman

$ FOLD3 <fold3.com>: records and every-name indexes for 1860, 1930 and portions of 1900–1920

HERITAGEQUEST ONLINE <www.heritagequestonline.com>: record images for all US censuses; head-of-household indexes for 1790–1820, 1860–1920 and part of 1930 (available through subscribing libraries)

USGENWEB ARCHIVES CENSUS PROJECT <usgwarchives.net/census>: volunteer-submitted indexes and some images of census records from various places and years

CENSUS SEARCH DO'S AND DON'TS

Mind these tips for more-effective searching of online census databases:

Do
- Experiment with the site's search tools, entering different search parameters and spellings.

- Look for search tips to see whether you can use tools such as wildcard symbols or Boolean searching to catch mistranscriptions and unexpected spellings.

- Try searching without a name—enter other information such as the person's place of residence, birth date and immigration date.

- Search for friends and neighbors your ancestor may have been living with.

Don't
- Expect to find an ancestor on the first try.

- Assume the site's data match everything you understand to be true about your family. Names may be spelled differently, for example, or people may have reported different ages or immigration dates from what you've found in other sources.

• Assume it's your ancestor because the name is right. Multiple people could've had the same name.

ONLINE CENSUS SEARCH TIPS

READ THE SITE'S SEARCH TIPS AND INSTRUCTIONS. They'll reveal tricks such as using wildcard symbols to find alternate spellings of your ancestors' names.

SEARCH A SITE'S INDIVIDUAL CENSUS DATABASES ONE AT A TIME. Those customized search forms often let you include terms not allowed in a site's global search, letting you better target your search.

MAKE SURE THE COLLECTION COVERS THE RIGHT TIME AND PLACE. Go to the page for the individual census database and look for background information. You might learn the collection doesn't contain all extant census schedules, or that the place where your ancestor lived wasn't indexed or wasn't included in that enumeration.

TRY DIFFERENT APPROACHES. Start by entering all you know about the person. If you don't get results, search on fewer terms and combinations of terms.

SEEK ALTERNATE NAME SPELLINGS. A census taker or an indexer might've interpreted the name so outlandishly that a "sounds like" search wouldn't pick up on the misspelling.

LEAVE OUT THE NAME. Instead of a name, search on variables such as residence, birth date and place, place of origin and immigration date.

BE FLEXIBLE. Your ancestor might've lived in a place you didn't expect, or he might have reported a different age or birthplace from the one you were looking for. Use date ranges and try leaving some fields blank to account for uncertainty.

BROWSE. Navigate to schedules for the census year and the enumeration district (ED) where you think your ancestor lived (you can use the ED tools at **<www.stevemorse.org>** to determine the enumeration district). Then examine the records page by page.

ENUMERATION DISTRICTS

DEFINITION: An enumeration district is a geographic area assigned to each census taker. The Census Bureau prepared maps of these districts for 1880 to 1970.

AREA: In most years, the census was taken by county. Within the county or other major civil division, many subdivisions may have been used, including township, precinct, city, town, village, district, division and ward.

WHERE TO FIND MAPS OF THE DISTRICTS:
National Archives micropublication T1224, *Descriptions of Census Enumeration Districts, 1830–1890 and 1910–1950* (146 rolls)

National Archives micropublication T1210, *Descriptions of Census Enumeration Districts, 1900* (10 rolls)

One-Step by Stephen Morse **<stevemorse.org/ed/ed.php>**

Family History Library **<familysearch.org>** has photocopies of the full-sized maps and maps on microfiche.

▷ Tips and tricks

• In some states and territories, county divisions were not clearly defined, have changed, were referred to by other names or may not have existed at all.

• The National Archives has no pre-1880 ED maps, and it has descriptions only for 1830 through 1870. Most early district descriptions are general and largely served as documentation of the names of enumerators and rates of pay.

• Check the Guide to Cartographic Records of the Bureau of the Census, compiled by James Berton Rhoads and Charlotte M. Ashby, for a description of enumeration district maps.

• If your ancestor wasn't a city dweller, you can locate the enumeration district for the 1880 to 1940 censuses at **<stevemorse.org/ed/ed.php>**.

• Search digitized enumeration district maps for the 1940 census at **<stevemorse.org/census/arc1940edmaps. html>**.

FINDING ADDRESSES

To effectively use the enumeration district maps, you need an address for the person as close to the census year as possible. This is particularly important when searching for city residents in the unindexed 1930 census. Addresses can be found in
• birth certificates
• census records for prior years
• city or county directories
• court records
• death certificates
• funeral home records
• heredity and lineage applications

- land and tax records
- letters and postcards
- marriage and divorce records
- military records
- naturalization and passenger arrival records
- oral interviews
- school records

FAMOUS NAMES IN CENSUSES

We found the following famous names in historical census returns:

BUZZ ALDRIN 1930 federal census (age 3 months as Edwin E Aldrin) 25 Princeton Place, Montclair Town, Essex County, New Jersey

HECTOR BOIARDI (CHEF BOY-AR-DEE) 1920 federal census (age 23) Ward 11, Cleveland, Ohio

LIZZIE BORDEN 1880 federal census (age 19) 92 Second St., Fall River, Bristol County, Massachusetts

AMELIA EARHART 1900 federal census (age 2) 1021 Ann Ave., Kansas City, Wyandotte County, Kansas; 1930 federal census (age 31, listed as a guest) 353–361 West 57th St., Manhattan, New York, New York

THOMAS EDISON 1850 federal census (age 3, recorded as Alana Edison, a misspelling of his middle name, Alva) Milan Township, Erie County, Ohio; 1930 federal census (age 62, recorded as Thomas A. Edison) Valley Road, West Orange Township, Essex County, New Jersey

HELEN KELLER 1900 federal census (age 19), Tuscumbia Precinct, Colbert County, Alabama

JOHN F. KENNEDY 1920 federal census (age 2½) 83 Beals St., Brookline, Norfolk County, Massachusetts

MARTIN LUTHER KING JR. 1930 federal census (age 1, as Marvin L. King Jr.), Ward 4, Atlanta Borough, Fulton County, Georgia

ABRAHAM LINCOLN 1850 federal census (age 40, recorded as Abram Lincoln) Springfield, Sangamon County, Illinois

ORVILLE WRIGHT 1880 federal census (age 8) 104 Greene St., Ward 2, Cedar Rapids, Iowa

WILBUR WRIGHT 1870 federal census (age 3) 12th Ward, Dayton, Ohio; 1880 federal census (age 13) 104 Greene St., Ward 2, Cedar Rapids, Iowa

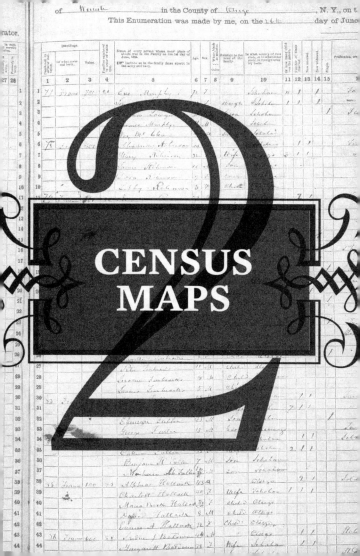

CENSUS MAPS

AREA ENUMERATED IN THE 1790 CENSUS

Connecticut
Delaware
District of Columbia
Georgia
Kentucky (as a district)
Maine (as a district)
Maryland
Massachusetts
New Hampshire
New Jersey
New York
North Carolina
Pennsylvania
Rhode Island
South Carolina
Tennessee (as Southwest Territory)
Vermont (as a district)
Virginia
West Virginia (as part of Virginia)

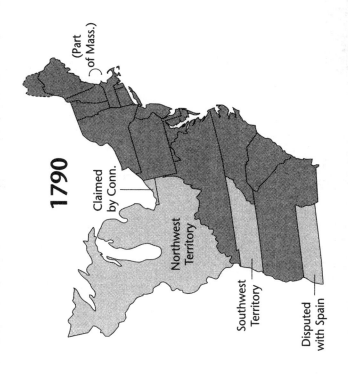

1790

(Part of Mass.)

Claimed by Conn.

Northwest Territory

Southwest Territory

Disputed with Spain

AREA ENUMERATED IN THE 1800 CENSUS

Alabama (as part of Mississippi Territory)
Connecticut
Delaware
District of Columbia
Georgia
Indiana (as part of Indiana Territory)
Kentucky
Maine (as a district)
Maryland
Massachusetts
Mississippi (as part of Mississippi Territory)
New Hampshire
New Jersey
New York
North Carolina
Ohio (as part of Indiana Territory)
Pennsylvania
Rhode Island
South Carolina
Tennessee
Vermont
Virginia
West Virginia (as part of Virginia)

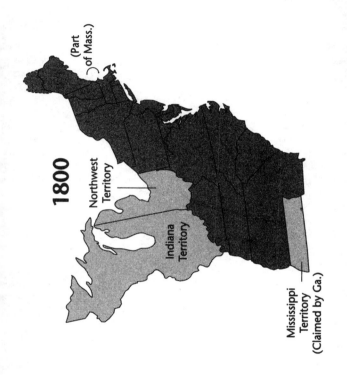

1800

(Part of Mass.)

Northwest Territory

Indiana Territory

Mississippi Territory (Claimed by Ga.)

AREA ENUMERATED IN THE 1810 CENSUS

Alabama (as part of Mississippi Territory)
Arkansas (as Louisiana Territory)
Connecticut
Delaware
District of Columbia
Georgia
Illinois (as Illinois Territory)
Indiana (as Indiana Territory)
Kentucky
Louisiana (as Orleans Territory)
Maine
Maryland
Massachusetts
Michigan (as Michigan Territory)
Mississippi (as part of Mississippi Territory)
Missouri (as Louisiana Territory)
New Hampshire
New Jersey
New York
North Carolina
Ohio
Pennsylvania
Rhode Island
South Carolina
Tennessee
Vermont
Virginia
West Virginia (as part of Virginia)

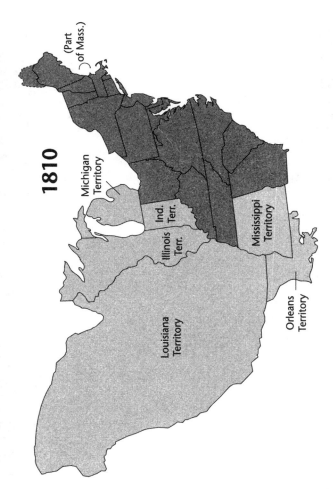

1810

(Part of Mass.)

Michigan Territory

Ind. Terr.

Illinois Terr.

Mississippi Territory

Louisiana Territory

Orleans Territory

AREA ENUMERATED IN THE 1820 CENSUS

Alabama
Arkansas (as Arkansas Territory)
Connecticut
Delaware
District of Columbia
Georgia
Illinois
Indiana
Kentucky
Louisiana
Maine
Maryland
Massachusetts
Michigan
Mississippi
Missouri (as Missouri Territory)
New Hampshire
New Jersey
New York
North Carolina
Ohio
Pennsylvania
Rhode Island
South Carolina
Tennessee
Vermont
Virginia
West Virginia (as part of Virginia)

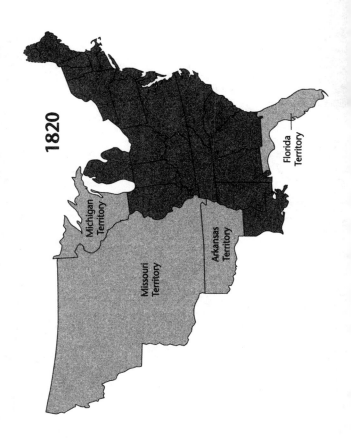

1820

Michigan
Territory

Missouri
Territory

Arkansas
Territory

Florida
Territory

AREA ENUMERATED IN THE 1830 CENSUS

Alabama
Arkansas (as Arkansas Territory)
Connecticut
Delaware
District of Columbia
Florida (as Florida Territory)
Georgia
Illinois
Indiana
Kentucky
Louisiana
Maine
Maryland
Massachusetts
Michigan
Mississippi
Missouri
New Hampshire
New Jersey
New York
North Carolina
Ohio
Pennsylvania
Rhode Island
South Carolina
Tennessee
Vermont
Virginia
West Virginia (as part of Virginia)

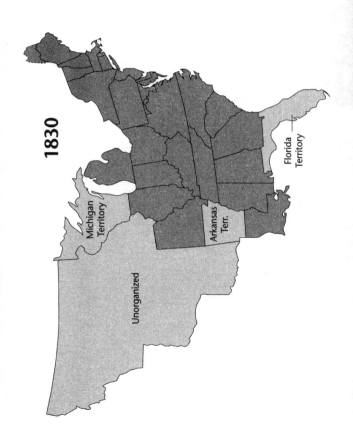

1830

Michigan Territory

Unorganized

Arkansas Terr.

Florida Territory

AREA ENUMERATED IN THE 1840 CENSUS

Alabama
Arkansas
Connecticut
Delaware
District of Columbia
Georgia
Florida (as Florida Territory)
Illinois
Indiana
Iowa (as Iowa Territory)
Kentucky
Louisiana
Maine
Maryland
Massachusetts
Michigan
Mississippi
Missouri
New Hampshire
New Jersey
New York
North Carolina
Ohio
Pennsylvania
Rhode Island
South Carolina
Tennessee
Vermont
Virginia
West Virginia (as part of Virginia)
Wisconsin (as Wisconsin Territory)

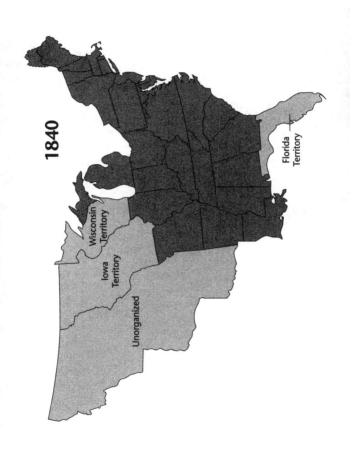

1840

Florida Territory

Wisconsin Territory

Iowa Territory

Unorganized

AREA ENUMERATED IN THE 1850 CENSUS

Alabama
Arkansas
California
Connecticut
Delaware
District of Columbia
Georgia
Florida
Illinois
Indiana
Iowa
Kentucky
Louisiana
Maine
Maryland
Massachusetts
Michigan
Minnesota (as Minnesota Territory)
Mississippi
Missouri
New Hampshire
New Jersey
New Mexico (as New Mexico Territory)
New York
North Carolina
Ohio
Oregon (as Oregon Territory)
Pennsylvania
Rhode Island
South Carolina
Tennessee
Texas
Utah (as Utah Territory)
Vermont
Virginia
Washington (as Oregon Territory)
West Virginia (as part of Virginia)
Wisconsin

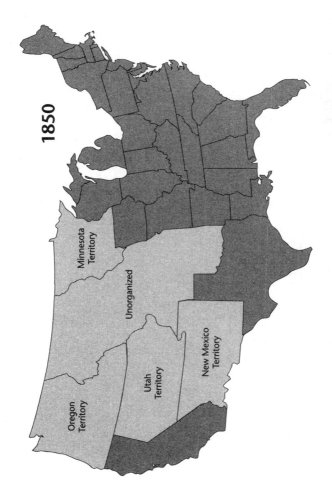

1850

Minnesota Territory

Unorganized

Oregon Territory

Utah Territory

New Mexico Territory

AREA ENUMERATED IN THE 1860 CENSUS

Alabama
Arizona (as New Mexico Territory)
Arkansas
California
Colorado (as Utah and Kansas territories)
Connecticut
Delaware
District of Columbia
Georgia
Florida
Illinois
Indiana
Iowa
Kansas (as Kansas Territory)
Kentucky
Louisiana
Maine
Maryland
Massachusetts
Michigan
Minnesota
Mississippi
Missouri
Nebraska (as Nebraska Territory)
Nevada (as Utah Territory)
New Hampshire
New Jersey
New Mexico (as New Mexico Territory)
New York
North Carolina
North Dakota (as Nebraska Territory)
Ohio
Oregon
Pennsylvania
Rhode Island
South Carolina
South Dakota (as Nebraska Territory)
Tennessee
Texas
Utah (as Utah Territory)
Vermont
Virginia
Washington (as Oregon Territory)
West Virginia (as part of Virginia)
Wisconsin

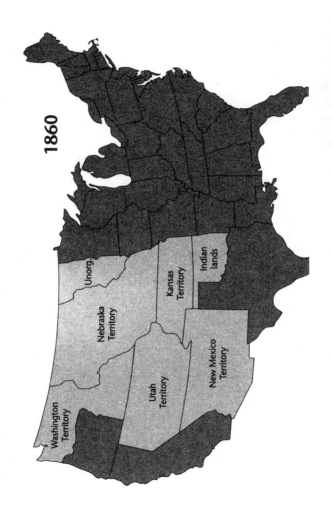

1860

Washington Territory

Nebraska Territory

Unorg.

Utah Territory

Kansas Territory

New Mexico Territory

Indian lands

AREA ENUMERATED IN THE 1870 CENSUS

Alabama
Arizona (as New Mexico Territory)
Arkansas
California
Colorado (as Colorado Territory)
Connecticut
Delaware
District of Columbia
Georgia
Florida
Idaho (as Idaho Territory)
Illinois
Indiana
Iowa
Kansas
Kentucky
Louisiana
Maine
Maryland
Massachusetts
Michigan
Minnesota
Mississippi
Missouri
Montana (as Montana Territory)
Nebraska
Nevada
New Hampshire
New Jersey
New Mexico (as New Mexico Territory)
New York
North Carolina
North Dakota (as Dakota Territory)
Ohio
Oregon
Pennsylvania
Rhode Island
South Carolina
South Dakota (as Dakota Territory)
Tennessee
Texas
Utah (as Utah Territory)
Vermont
Virginia
Washington (as Washington Territory)
West Virginia
Wisconsin
Wyoming (as Wyoming Territory)

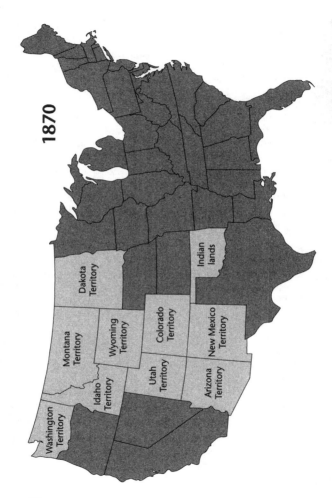

1870

Washington Territory

Montana Territory

Idaho Territory

Dakota Territory

Wyoming Territory

Utah Territory

Colorado Territory

New Mexico Territory

Arizona Territory

Indian lands

AREA ENUMERATED IN THE 1880 CENSUS

Alabama
Alaska (as a territory)
Arizona (as New Mexico Territory)
Arkansas
California
Colorado
Connecticut
Delaware
District of Columbia
Georgia
Florida
Idaho (as Idaho Territory)
Illinois
Indiana
Iowa
Kansas
Kentucky
Louisiana
Maine
Maryland
Massachusetts
Michigan
Minnesota
Mississippi
Missouri
Montana (as Montana Territory)
Nebraska
Nevada
New Hampshire
New Jersey
New Mexico (as New Mexico Territory)
New York
North Carolina
North Dakota (as Dakota Territory)
Ohio
Oregon
Pennsylvania
Rhode Island
South Carolina
South Dakota (as Dakota Territory)
Tennessee
Texas
Utah (as Utah Territory)
Vermont
Virginia
Washington (as Washington Territory)
West Virginia
Wisconsin
Wyoming (as Wyoming Territory)

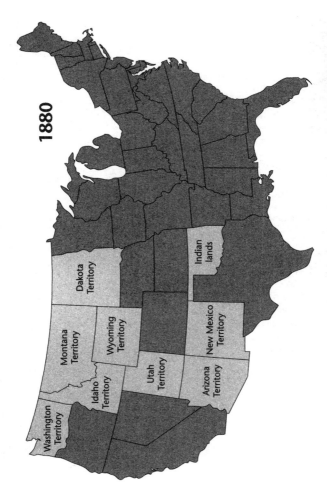

1880

Washington Territory

Montana Territory

Idaho Territory

Dakota Territory

Wyoming Territory

Utah Territory

Arizona Territory

New Mexico Territory

Indian lands

AREA ENUMERATED IN THE 1890 CENSUS

Alabama
Alaska (as a territory)
Arizona (as New Mexico Territory)
Arkansas
California
Colorado
Connecticut
Delaware
District of Columbia
Georgia
Florida
Idaho
Illinois
Indiana
Iowa
Kansas
Kentucky
Louisiana
Maine
Maryland
Massachusetts
Michigan
Minnesota
Mississippi
Missouri
Montana

Nebraska
Nevada
New Hampshire
New Jersey
New Mexico (as New Mexico Territory)
New York
North Carolina
North Dakota
Ohio
Oklahoma (as Oklahoma Territory)
Oregon
Pennsylvania
Rhode Island
South Carolina
South Dakota
Tennessee
Texas
Utah (as Utah Territory)
Vermont
Virginia
Washington
West Virginia
Wisconsin
Wyoming

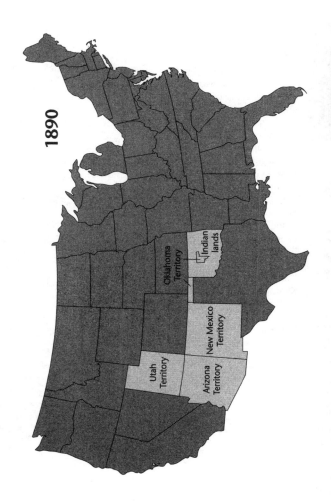

1890

Oklahoma Territory

Indian lands

New Mexico Territory

Utah Territory

Arizona Territory

AREA ENUMERATED IN THE 1900 CENSUS

Alabama
Alaska (as a territory)
Arizona (as New Mexico Territory)
Arkansas
California
Colorado
Connecticut
Delaware
District of Columbia
Georgia
Florida
Hawaii (as a territory)
Idaho
Illinois
Indiana
Iowa
Kansas
Kentucky
Louisiana
Maine
Maryland
Massachusetts
Michigan
Minnesota
Mississippi
Missouri
Montana
Nebraska
Nevada
New Hampshire
New Jersey
New Mexico (as New Mexico Territory)
New York
North Carolina
North Dakota
Ohio
Oklahoma (as Oklahoma Territory)
Oregon
Pennsylvania
Rhode Island
South Carolina
South Dakota
Tennessee
Texas
Utah (as Utah Territory)
Vermont
Virginia
Washington
West Virginia
Wisconsin
Wyoming

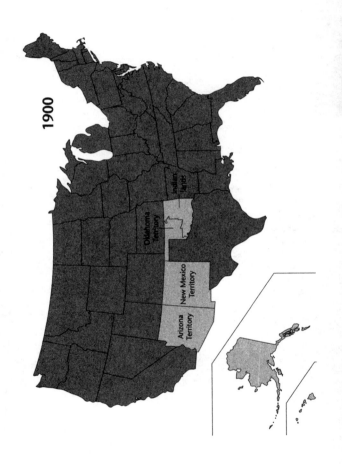

1900

Oklahoma Territory

Indian Lands

New Mexico Territory

Arizona Territory

AREA ENUMERATED IN THE 1910 CENSUS

Alabama
Alaska (as a territory)
Arizona (as New Mexico Territory)
Arkansas
California
Colorado
Connecticut
Delaware
District of Columbia
Georgia
Florida
Hawaii (as a territory)
Idaho
Illinois
Indiana
Iowa
Kansas
Kentucky
Louisiana
Maine
Maryland
Massachusetts
Michigan
Minnesota
Mississippi
Missouri
Montana
Nebraska
Nevada
New Hampshire
New Jersey
New Mexico (as New Mexico Territory)
New York
North Carolina
North Dakota
Ohio
Oklahoma
Oregon
Pennsylvania
Puerto Rico
Rhode Island
South Carolina
South Dakota
Tennessee
Texas
Utah (as Utah Territory)
Vermont
Virginia
Washington
West Virginia
Wisconsin
Wyoming

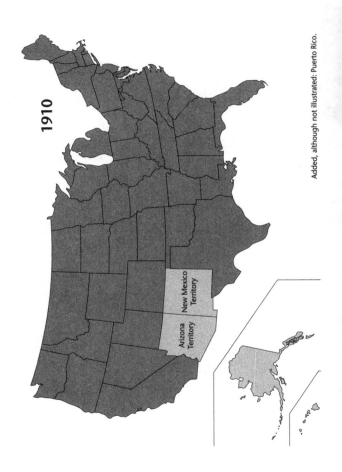

1910

New Mexico Territory

Arizona Territory

Added, although not illustrated: Puerto Rico.

AREA ENUMERATED IN THE 1920 CENSUS

Alabama
Alaska (as a territory)
Arizona
Arkansas
California
Colorado
Connecticut
Delaware
District of Columbia
Georgia
Guam
Florida
Hawaii (as a territory)
Idaho
Illinois
Indiana
Iowa
Kansas
Kentucky
Louisiana
Maine
Maryland
Massachusetts
Michigan
Minnesota
Mississippi
Missouri
Montana
Nebraska
Nevada
New Hampshire
New Jersey
New Mexico
New York
North Carolina
North Dakota
Ohio
Oklahoma
Oregon
Panama Canal Zone
Pennsylvania
Puerto Rico
Rhode Island
Samoa
South Carolina
South Dakota
Tennessee
Texas
Utah (as Utah Territory)
Vermont
Virgin Island
Virginia
Washington
West Virginia
Wisconsin
Wyoming

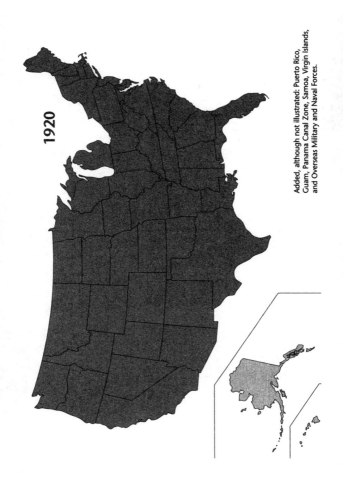

1920

Added, although not illustrated: Puerto Rico, Guam, Panama Canal Zone, Samoa, Virgin Islands, and Overseas Military and Naval Forces.

AREA ENUMERATED IN THE 1930 CENSUS

Alabama
Alaska (as a territory)
Arizona
Arkansas
California
Colorado
Connecticut
Delaware
District of Columbia
Georgia
Guam
Florida
Hawaii (as a territory)
Idaho
Illinois
Indiana
Iowa
Kansas
Kentucky
Louisiana
Maine
Maryland
Massachusetts
Michigan
Minnesota
Mississippi
Missouri
Montana

Nebraska
Nevada
New Hampshire
New Jersey
New Mexico
New York
North Carolina
North Dakota
Ohio
Oklahoma
Oregon
Panama Canal Zone
Pennsylvania
Puerto Rico
Rhode Island
Samoa
South Carolina
South Dakota
Tennessee
Texas
Utah (as Utah Territory)
Vermont
Virginia
Washington
West Virginia
Wisconsin
Wyoming

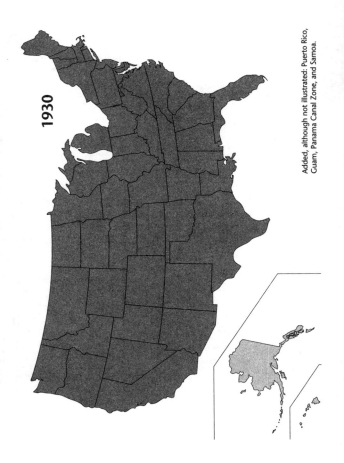

1930

Added, although not illustrated: Puerto Rico, Guam, Panama Canal Zone, and Samoa.

AREA ENUMERATED IN THE 1940 CENSUS

Alabama
Alaska (as a territory)
Arizona
Arkansas
California
Colorado
Connecticut
Delaware
District of Columbia
Georgia
Guam
Florida
Hawaii (as a territory)
Idaho
Illinois
Indiana
Iowa
Kansas
Kentucky
Louisiana
Maine
Maryland
Massachusetts
Michigan
Minnesota
Mississippi
Missouri
Montana

Nebraska
Nevada
New Hampshire
New Jersey
New Mexico
New York
North Carolina
North Dakota
Ohio
Oklahoma
Oregon
Panama Canal Zone
Pennsylvania
Puerto Rico
Rhode Island
Samoa
South Carolina
South Dakota
Tennessee
Texas
Utah (as Utah Territory)
Vermont
Virginia
Washington
West Virginia
Wisconsin
Wyoming

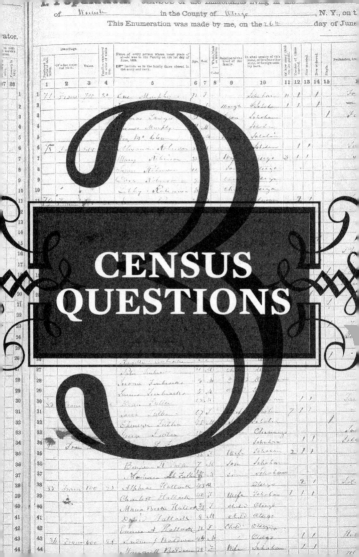

CENSUS QUESTIONS

1790 CENSUS

The nation's first head count was as genealogically bare bones as could be: If you find an ancestral family in the 1790 census, the result will be nothing more than a name and a line of numbers. Enumerators recorded the name of the head of the family and the number of household members falling into demographic categories.

▷ **1790 census questions**
• Name of head of family
• Free white males 16 years and older, including heads of family
• Free white males under 16 years
• Free white females
• All other free persons
• Slaves
• Dwellings and miscellaneous

1800 AND 1810 CENSUSES

The next two censuses, which used identical questionnaires, broke down the ages of household members in greater detail. For both free white males and free white females, these censuses counted those under age 10, 10 and under 16, 16 and under 26, 26 and under 45, and age 45 and up, as well as other free persons and slaves.

This breakdown is far more useful than the one in 1790, because it can help to separate parents from children (or grandparents living with their adult children and grandchildren) and it lets you match up the offspring more accurately.

▷ **1800 and 1810 census questions**
• Name of head of family
• Number of free white males under age 10
• Number of free white males of 10 and under 16

- Number of free white males of 16 and under 26
- Number of free white males of 26 and under 45
- Number of free white males of 45 and up
- Number of free white females under age 10
- Number of free white females of 10 and under 16
- Number of free white females of 16 and under 26
- Number of free white females of 26 and under 45
- Number of free white females of 45 and up
- Number of all other persons except Indians not taxed
- Number of slaves

1820 CENSUS

The 1820 census kept the same age and gender categories as the previous two except for an added column breaking out males ages 16 to 18 (who were double-counted under males age 16 to 26). This can really narrow a birth year if you happen to have a male ancestor born about 1802 to 1804. Just keep in mind that all age questions were supposed to be answered as of the date the enumeration began: Aug. 7, 1820. This census also asked for the number of "Foreigners not naturalized" and those engaged in agriculture, commerce and manufacturing. Important for those with African-American ancestors, 1820 was the first census to distinguish between slaves and "free colored," who were enumerated by gender and age (to age 14, 14 to 26, 26 to 45, and 45 and up).

▷ **1820 census questions**
- Name of head of family
- Number of free white males under age 10
- Number of free white males 10 to 16
- Number of free white males 16 to 18
- Number of free white males 16 to 26
- Number of free white males 26 to 45
- Number of free white males 45 and up
- Number of free white females under age 10

- Number of free white females 10 to 16
- Number of free white females 16 to 26
- Number of free white females 26 to 45
- Number of free white females 45 and up
- Number of foreigners not naturalized
- Number of persons engaged in agriculture
- Number of persons engaged in commerce
- Number of persons engaged in manufacturing
- Number of free colored males to age 14
- Number of free colored males 14 to 26
- Number of free colored males 26 to 45
- Number of free colored males 45 and up
- Number of free colored females to age 14
- Number of free colored females 14 to 26
- Number of free colored females 26 to 45
- Number of free colored females 45 and up
- All other persons
- Slaves

1830 AND 1840 CENSUSES

The 1830 enumeration—the first to use a standardized form—and the similar 1840 questionnaire broke down ages even more finely: under 5, 5 to 10, 10 to 15, 15 to 20, and every 10 years to the novel "Over 100." (Ages were reported as of June 1 for both censuses.) A second page of the form recorded both slaves and "free colored" by gender and age: under 10, 10 to 24, 24 to 36, 36 to 55, 55 to 100, and 100 and up. There's again a count of non-naturalized white foreigners. New questions asked about persons who were deaf and dumb, separated by white, slaves and free colored; and by age (under 14, 14 to 25, and 25 and up). Blind household members also were counted, but weren't differentiated.

▷ 1830 census questions

Page 1
- Name of head of family
- Number of free white males under age 5
- Number of free white males age 5 to 10
- Number of free white males age 10 to 15
- Number of free white males age 15 to 20
- Number of free white males age 20 to 30
- Number of free white males age 30 to 40
- Number of free white males age 40 to 50
- Number of free white males age 50 to 60
- Number of free white males age 60 to 70
- Number of free white males age 70 to 80
- Number of free white males age 80 to 90
- Number of free white males age 90 to 100
- Number of free white males age 100 and up
- Number of free white females under age 5
- Number of free white females age 5 to 10
- Number of free white females age 10 to 15
- Number of free white females age 15 to 20
- Number of free white females age 20 to 30
- Number of free white females age 30 to 40
- Number of free white females age 40 to 50
- Number of free white females age 50 to 60
- Number of free white females age 60 to 70
- Number of free white females age 70 to 80
- Number of free white females age 80 to 90
- Number of free white females age 90 to 100
- Number of free white females age 100 and up

Page 2
- Name of head of family
- Number of male slaves under age 10
- Number of male slaves age 10 to 24
- Number of male slaves age 24 to 36
- Number of male slaves age 36 to 55

- Number of male slaves age 55 to 100
- Number of male slaves age 100 and up
- Number of female slaves under age 10
- Number of female slaves age 10 to 24
- Number of female slaves age 24 to 36
- Number of female slaves age 36 to 55
- Number of female slaves age 55 to 100
- Number of female slaves age 100 and up
- Number of free colored males under age 10
- Number of free colored males age 10 to 24
- Number of free colored males age 24 to 36
- Number of free colored males age 36 to 55
- Number of free colored males age 55 to 100
- Number of free colored males age 100 and up
- Number of free colored females under age 10
- Number of free colored females age 10 to 24
- Number of free colored females age 24 to 36
- Number of free colored females age 36 to 55
- Number of free colored females age 55 to 100
- Number of free colored females age 100 and up

Total
- White persons deaf and dumb under age 14
- White persons deaf and dumb age 14 to 25
- White persons deaf and dumb age 25 and up
- White persons blind
- White foreigners not naturalized
- Slaves and colored persons deaf and dumb under age 14
- Slaves and colored persons deaf and dumb age 14 to 25
- Slaves and colored persons deaf and dumb age 25 and up
- Slaves and colored persons persons blind

▷ 1840 census questions
Page 1
- Name of head of family
- Number of free white males under age 5

- Number of free white males age 5 to 10
- Number of free white males age 10 to 15
- Number of free white males age 15 to 20
- Number of free white males age 20 to 30
- Number of free white males age 30 to 40
- Number of free white males age 40 to 50
- Number of free white males age 50 to 60
- Number of free white males age 60 to 70
- Number of free white males age 70 to 80
- Number of free white males age 80 to 90
- Number of free white males age 90 to 100
- Number of free white males age 100 and up
- Number of free white females under age 5
- Number of free white females age 5 to 10
- Number of free white females age 10 to 15
- Number of free white females age 15 to 20
- Number of free white females age 20 to 30
- Number of free white females age 30 to 40
- Number of free white females age 40 to 50
- Number of free white females age 50 to 60
- Number of free white females age 60 to 70
- Number of free white females age 70 to 80
- Number of free white females age 80 to 90
- Number of free white females age 90 to 100
- Number of free white females age 100 and up

Page 2
- Name of head of family
- Number of male slaves under age 10
- Number of male slaves age 10 to 24
- Number of male slaves age 24 to 36
- Number of male slaves age 36 to 55
- Number of male slaves age 55 to 100
- Number of male slaves age 100 and up
- Number of female slaves under age 10
- Number of female slaves age 10 to 24

- Number of female slaves age 24 to 36
- Number of female slaves age 36 to 55
- Number of female slaves age 55 to 100
- Number of female slaves age 100 and up
- Number of free colored males under age 10
- Number of free colored males age 10 to 24
- Number of free colored males age 24 to 36
- Number of free colored males age 36 to 55
- Number of free colored males age 55 to 100
- Number of free colored males age 100 and up
- Number of free colored females under age 10
- Number of free colored females age 10 to 24
- Number of free colored females age 24 to 36
- Number of free colored females age 36 to 55
- Number of free colored females age 55 to 100
- Number of free colored females age 100 and up

Total
- Number of persons employed in mining
- Number of persons employed in agriculture
- Number of persons employed in commerce
- Number of persons employed in manufacturing and trades
- Number of persons employed in ocean navigation
- Number of persons employed in canal, lake, river navigation
- Number of persons employed in learned prof'ns and engineers
- Revolutionary or military service pensioner's name
- Revolutionary or military service pensioner's age

1850 AND 1860 CENSUSES
The 1850 census was the first to list each free person in the household by name, and specific ages (as of June 1) replaced those frustrating ranges. Each person was asked for birthplace (state or territory). Other questions covered sex, color, occupation, value of real estate, whether married within the year,

attending school within the year, illiteracy and whether "deaf and dumb, blind, insane, idiot, pauper or convict." This was also the first census to have separate schedules for slaves and for people who'd died in the year prior to the census, called mortality schedules; they also exist for the 1860, 1870 and 1880 censuses.

The 1860 census questions were essentially the same as a decade before. It's notable, especially for Southern ancestors, as the last census before the disruptions of the Civil War, and it of course included the last slave schedule.

▷ **1850 census questions**
1. Dwelling number
2. Family number
3. Name of every person whose usual place of abode on June 1, 1850 was with this family
4. Age
5. Sex
6. Color
7. Profession, occupation or trade of each male over 15
8. Value of real estate owned
9. Place of birth
10. Married within the year
11. In school within the year
12. Persons over 20 unable to read and write
13. If deaf and dumb, blind, insane, idiot, pauper or convict

▷ **1850 census slave schedule**
• Name of slave owners
• Number of slaves
• Age
• Sex
• Color
• Fugitives from the state
• Number manumitted

- Deaf and dumb, blind, insane or idiotic
- Number of slave houses

▷ 1860 census questions

1. Dwelling number
2. Family number
3. Name of every person whose usual place of abode on June 1, 1860 was with this family
4. Age
5. Sex
6. Color
7. Profession, occupation or trade of each male over 15
8. Value of real estate owned
9. Value of personal estate owned
10. Place of birth
11. Married within the year
12. In school within the year
13. Persons over 20 unable to read and write
14. If deaf and dumb, blind, insane, idiot, pauper or convict

▷ 1860 census slave schedule questions

- Name of slave owners
- Number of slaves
- Age
- Sex
- Color
- Fugitives from the state
- Number manumitted
- Deaf and dumb, blind, insane or idiotic
- Number of slave houses

1870 CENSUS

This was the first census to count all individuals as "whole persons," the 14th Amendment having abolished the three-fifths counting rule in 1868. Similar to the 1850 and 1860 questionnaires, the 1870 census again included age (as of June 1) and birthplace. For the first time, it asked yes-or-no questions about whether each person's parents were foreign-born. Another two easily missed columns asked for the month of birth for babies born within the year and for the month of marriage for couples wed within the year.

▷ **1870 census questions**
1. Dwelling number
2. Family number
3. Name of every person whose usual place of abode on June 1, 1870 was with this family
4. Age
5. Sex
6. Color
7. Profession, occupation or trade
8. Value of real estate owned
9. Value of personal estate owned
10. Place of birth
11. Father foreign-born
12. Mother foreign-born
13. Month born within the year
14. Month married within the year
15. In school within the year
16. Cannot read
17. Cannot write
18. Deaf and dumb, blind, insane or idiotic
19. Males eligible to vote
20. Males not eligible to vote

1880 CENSUS

Besides asking the individual's birthplace, questions also asked the birthplaces of the person's father and mother. Here again, the 1880 enumeration lets you reach back in time, providing answers that were missing from earlier forms.

The 1880 questionnaire also added the genealogically important question of each person's relationship to the head of household. You might assume that everybody in the family is a spouse, son or daughter of the head of household, but often nieces, nephews, grandparents and other kin moved in with relatives. Thanks to the 1880 questionnaire, you can figure out who's who. Similarly and perhaps surprisingly, 1880 was the first census to specifically ask marital status, with columns for single, married and widowed/divorced. It also asked whether married within the census year, but not for the month.

▷ **1880 census questions**
Street name
House number
1. Dwelling number
2. Family number
3. Name of every person whose usual place of abode on June 1, 1880 was with this family
4. Color
5. Sex
6. Age
7. Month born if during census year
8. Relationship to head of household
9. Single
10. Married
11. Widowed/divorced
12. Married during year
13. Profession, occupation or trade
14. Months unemployed this year
15. Currently ill? If so, specify.

16. Blind
17. Deaf and dumb
18. Idiotic
19. Insane
20. Disabled
21. School this year
22. Cannot read
23. Cannot write
24. Birthplace
25. Birthplace of father
26. Birthplace of mother

1890 CENSUS

Lost to fire except for fragments, the 1890 forms adopted a dramatically different, vertical look and added questions about how long a person had lived in the United States and his or her naturalization status. This enumeration also included the column "mother of how many children" and how many of those children were living. The 1890 census included a veterans schedule for enumerating Union veterans of the Civil War (although some Confederates were also counted) and their widows; about half of these schedules survived and can substitute for the lost census if you're lucky enough to have a Union soldier in the family.

1900 CENSUS

For the first and only time among available censuses, enumerators asked adults for their month and year of birth. If an ancestor was recorded in 1900, you can finally resolve those nagging questions from other censuses about approximated ages. The 1900 form added a question about number of years married and was the first census to ask about home ownership—owned or rented, and owned free or mortgaged.

Another 1900 first: Enumerators asked for the year a person immigrated to the United States. Given the loss of the 1890 returns, with their question about how long a person had been in the country, 1900 represents your earliest opportunity to let the census nail down that elusive "crossing the pond" year. Armed with this fact, you can narrow your passenger records search.

▷ 1900 census questions

Street

House number

1. Dwelling number
2. Family number
3. Name of every person whose usual place of abode on June 1, 1900 was with this family
4. Relationship to head of family
5. Color
6. Sex
7. Birth month and year
8. Age
9. Marital status
10. Number of years married
11. Mother of how many children?
12. Number of these children living
13. Birthplace of this person
14. Birthplace of this person's father
15. Birthplace of this person's mother
16. Year of immigration
17. Number of years in US
18. Naturalized citizen
19. Occupation of every person 10 and older
20. Months not employed
21. Months in school
22. Can read
23. Can write
24. Speaks English

25. Owned or rented
26. Owned free or mortgage
27. Farm or house
28. Number of farm schedule

1910 CENSUS

The census took a step backward, genealogically speaking, in 1910, losing the question about a person's month and year of birth because most states kept vital records by this time. It again asked for the year of immigration, a useful double-check on the previous census. The redundant "Number of years in US" question was dropped. For the first time, enumerators were supposed to ask about the mother tongue of foreign-born people, squeezing in an abbreviation for the answer next to the person's native country.

Don't overlook column 30 at the far right side of the form. All males over age 50 who were born in the United States or who immigrated before 1865 were asked whether they were "a survivor of the Union or Confederate Army or Navy." UA means Union Army, UN is for Union Navy, CA for Confederate Army and CN for Confederate Navy. If your ancestor answered that he served in the Union forces, look for him in the 1890 veterans schedules.

▷ **1910 census questions**
Street
Home number
1. Dwelling number
2. Family number
3. Name of every person whose usual place of abode on 15 April 1910 was with this family
4. Relationship
5. Sex
6. Color

7. Age
8. Marital status
9. Number of years—present marriage
10. Mother of how many children?
11. Number of living children
12. Birthplace of this person
13. Birthplace of this person's father
14. Birthplace of this person's mother
15. Year of immigration
16. Naturalized citizen or alien?
17. Speak English? If not, give name of language.
18. Profession or occupation
19. Nature of business
20. Employer or wage earner or working on own account
21. Out of work 15 April 1910
22. No. of weeks out of work in 1909
23. Can read
24. Can write
25. School since 1 September 1909
26. Owned/rented
27. Owned free or mortgaged
28. Farm or house
29. No. of farm schedule
30. Civil War veteran
31. Blind
32. Deaf and dumb

1920 CENSUS

The 1920 form closely followed 1910's with an additional question about a year of naturalization. "Mother tongue" got its own column for each person, and for each person's mother and father—no more squeezed-in squiggles. But "number of years married" was dropped from the form.

▷ 1920 census questions

1. Street
2. Home number
3. Dwelling number
4. Family number
5. Name of each person whore place of abode on 1 Jan. 1920 was in this family
6. Relationship
7. Own or rent home
8. Owned free or mortgaged
9. Sex
10. Color or race
11. Age
12. Marital status
13. Immigration year
14. Naturalized or alien
15. Naturalization year
16. School since 1 Sept. 1919
17. Can read
18. Can write
19. Birthplace of this person
20. Mother tongue
21. Birthplace of father
22. Mother tongue
23. Birthplace of mother
24. Mother tongue
25. Speaks English?
26. Profession or occupation
27. Nature of business
28. Employer, wage earner or self-employed
29. Number of farm schedule

1930 CENSUS

The 1930 census, the most recent available under federal privacy regulations, had the largest form yet, measuring 23¾ × 16½ inches, with several new questions of genealogical interest. "Age at first marriage" now followed "Marital condition." Two questions asked about a person's veteran status: whether a veteran and, if so, "what war or expedition." The year of naturalization was dropped.

This was also the first census to inquire whether the household had a "radio set." In another sign of the times, the standard population schedule was supplemented by a special "Census of Unemployment" (unfortunately, officials destroyed these schedules after collecting the data). There was also a short supplemental Indian schedule in 1930.

▷ **1930 census questions**
1. Street
2. Home number
3. Dwelling number
4. Family number
5. Name of every person whose place of abode on 1 April 1930 was in this family
6. Relationship to head of family
7. Own or rent home
8. Value of home or monthly rental
9. Radio set
10. Does family live on a farm?
11. Sex
12. Color or race
13. Age at last birthday
14. Marital condition
15. Age at first marriage
16. School since 1 September 1929
17. Can read and write
18. Birthplace of this person
19. Birthplace of this person's father
20. Birthplace of this person's mother
21. Language spoken in home before coming to US
22. Immigration year

23. Naturalization
24. Speaks English?
25. Occupation
26. Industry
27. Class of worker
28. Actually at work yesterday or last working day?
29. Line number for unemployed
30. Veteran?
31. Which war or expedition
32. Number of farm schedule

1940 CENSUS

Enumerators asked 34 questions, with ages given as of April 1, 1940. First came address and housing data, including whether the home was owned (O) or rented (R) and the value of the home or the monthly rent. Each person was listed by name, relationship to the head of household, sex, color or race, age at last birthday, marital status, education (whether attending school at any time since March 1, 1940, and the highest grade completed), and places of birth and citizenship (if foreign born). In recognition of the ways the war in Europe had already redrawn the map by 1940, foreign birthplaces were to reflect the "country in which the birthplace was situated on January 1, 1937." The remaining questions focused on the respondent's place of residence as of April 1, 1935 (a nifty way to track your relatives between censuses), employment and income.

Alas, only a randomly selected 5 percent of the population had to answer questions 35 through 50. This supplemental form—the Census Bureau's first use of statistical sampling—included such family history favorites as parents' birthplaces, mother tongue, veteran status, a woman's age at marriage and the number of children she'd given birth to. If your ancestor's name happened to fall on line 14 or 29 of the 40-entry enumeration sheet, you're in luck: Those persons got asked the supplemental questions.

▷ **1940 census questions**
1. Street
2. House number
3. Family number
4. Home owned or rented
5. Value of home if owned or monthly rental if rented
6. Does this household live on a farm
7. Name of each person whose usual place of residence on April 1, 1940, was in this household
8. Relation to head of household
9. Sex
10. Color or race
11. Age at last birthday
12. Marital status
13. Attended school or college any time since March 1, 1940?
14. Highest grade of school completed
15. Place of birth
16. Citizenship of the foreign born
17. City, town or village
18. County
19. State (or territory or foreign country)
20. On a farm?
21. Was this person at work for pay or profit in private or nonemergency government work during week of March 24–30?
22. If not, was he at work on or assigned to public emergency work (WPA, NYA, CCC, etc.) during week of March 24–30?
23. Was this person seeking work?
24. If not seeking work, did he have a job, business, etc.?
25. Indicate whether engaged in home housework, in school, unable to work or other

26. If at private or nonemergency work, number of hours worked during week of March 24–30?

27. If seeking work or assigned to public emergency work, duration of unemployment up to March 30, 1940—in weeks

28. Occupation

29. Industry

30. Class of worker

31. Number of weeks worked in 1939

32. Amount of money wages or salary received (including commissions)

33. Did this person receive income of $350 or more from sources other than money wages or salary?

34. Number of farm schedule

35. Name

36. Place of Birth of Father

37. Place of Birth of Mother

38. Mother Tongue

39. Veteran

40. If child, is veteran-father dead (yes or no)

41. War or Military service

42. Does this person have a Federal Social Security Number?

43. Were deductions for Federal Old-Age Insurance or Railroad Retirement made from this person's wages or salary in 1939?

44. If so, were deductions made from (1) all, (2) one-half or more, (3) part but less than half of wages or salary

45. Usual Occupation

46. Usual Industry

47. Usual class of worker

48. Has this woman been married more than once?

49. Age at first marriage

50. Number of children ever born

CENSUS QUESTIONS BY CATEGORY

▷ Name
• Head of Household: 1790, 1800, 1810, 1820, 1830, 1840
• Everyone in the Household (except slaves): from 1850 on

▷ Birth Date and Place
• Age Range of Free White Males (ranges differ): 1790, 1800, 1810, 1820, 1830, 1840
• Age Range of Free White Females (ranges differ): 1800, 1810, 1820, 1830, 1840
• Age of Everyone in the Household: 1850 on
• Birthplace: 1850 on
• Born Within the Census Year (with month): 1870, 1880
• Month and Year of Birth: 1900

▷ Parents
• Foreign-born Parents: 1870
• Parents' Place of Birth: 1880 on
• Mother Tongue: 1910
• Self and Parents' Mother Tongue: 1920, 1930

▷ Marriage
• Married Within the Census Year: 1850, 1860, 1870 (includes the month), 1880, 1890
• Marital Status: 1880 on
• Number of Years Married: 1900, 1910
• Age at First Marriage: 1930

▷ Immigration and Citizenship
• Number of Aliens/Persons not Naturalized: 1820, 1830, 1840
• Year of Immigration to the United States: 1900, 1910, 1920, 1930
• Number of Years in the United States: 1890, 1900
• Naturalization Status: 1870 (for males over 21), 1890, 1900, 1910, 1920, 1930

▷ Physical or Mental Health
- Persons in Household who Were Blind, Deaf or Dumb: 1830, 1840, 1850, 1860, 1870, 1880, 1890, 1910
- Persons in Household who Were Idiotic or Insane: 1850, 1860
- Mother of how Many Children/Number Living: 1890, 1900, 1910
- Whether Suffering From Chronic Disease: 1890

▷ Personal Property
- Value of Real Estate Owned: 1850, 1860, 1870
- Value of Personal Estate: 1860, 1870
- Own or Rent Home: 1900, 1910, 1920, 1930
- Had a Radio: 1930

▷ Education/Occupation
- Number of Persons (including slaves) Engaged in Agriculture, Commerce or Manufacturing: 1820
- Occupation: 1840 on
- Attended School in the Past Year: 1840 on
- Can Read or Write: 1850 on

▷ Other
- Number of Free Colored: 1820, 1830, 1840
- Color/Race: 1850 on
- Relationship to Head of Household: 1880 on
- Able to Speak English: 1900, 1910, 1920, 1930
- Veteran Status: 1890, 1910 (Civil War only), 1930
- Pensioner for Revolutionary War or Military Service: 1840
- If Person Is a Pauper, Convict or Homeless Child: 1850, 1860, 1890

1920 AND 1930 CENSUSES: FOREIGN LANGUAGES

Enumerators were given the following list of foreign languages that were likely to be reported in the 1920 and 1930 censuses as the mother tongue or native language of foreign-born persons. Use these responses as a clue to your ancestor's country of origin.

ALBANIAN: Indo-European language of Albania

ARABIC: a Semitic language, consisting of numerous dialects, that is the principal language of Arabia, Jordan, Syria, Iraq, Lebanon, Egypt and parts of northern Africa

ARMENIAN: Indo-European language of Armenia

BASQUE: language of Basques, of no known linguistic affiliation. The Basques are a people of unknown origin inhabiting the western Pyrenees in France and Spain.

BOHEMIAN: see Czech

BRETON: Celtic language of Brittany, a region of northwestern France

BULGARIAN: Slavic language of Bulgaria

CHINESE: any dialect spoken by Chinese people

CROATIAN: Slavic language of Croatia

CZECH: Slavic language of the Czechs, who are defined as natives or inhabitants of Czechoslovakia, especially Bohemians, Moravians or Slovaks

DALMATIAN: language of Dalmatia, a seaside region of Croatia

DANISH: North Germanic language of Denmark

DUTCH: West Germanic language of the Netherlands

EGYPTIAN: language of Egypt

ENGLISH: West Germanic language of England, the United States and other countries that are or have been under English influence or control

ESTONIAN: Finno-Ugric language of Estonia

FINNISH: Finno-Ugric language of Finland

FLEMISH: Low German language of Flemings, natives of Flanders or a Belgian who speaks Flemish

FRENCH: Romance language of France, Switzerland, parts of Belguim and other countries formerly under French control

FRISIAN: West Germanic language of the Frisian Islands or Friesland

FUJIAN: dialect of Chinese spoken in Fujian Province, eastern Guangdong Province and Taiwan

GAELIC: language of Scotland, Ireland and the Isle of Man

GEORGIAN: language of former Soviet Georgia

GERMAN: West Germanic language of Germany, Austria and part of Switzerland

GREAT RUSSIAN: language of central and northeastern Russia

GREEK: Indo-European language of Greece

GYPSY: Indic language of Gypsies

HEBREW: Semitic language of the ancient Hebrews or later forms of this language, especially the language of the Israelis

HINDI: language spoken in India, especially northern India

ICELANDIC: North Germanic language of Iceland

IRISH: language of Ireland

ITALIAN: Romance language of Italy and one of the three official languages of Switzerland

JAPANESE: language of Japan

KOREAN: language of Korea

KURDISH: Iranian language of the Kurds

LAPPISH: Finno-Ugric language of Lapland

LETTISH: Baltic language of the Latvians

LITHUANIAN: Baltic language of Lithuania

LITTLE RUSSIAN: East Slavic language spoken in Ukraine and in Ukrainian communities in neighboring Belarus, Russia, Poland and Slovakia

MACEDONIAN: Slavic language of modern Macedonia

MAGYAR: Finno-Ugric language of the Magyars. It is the official language of Hungary.

MONTENEGRIN: language of Montenegro, a Slavonic principality on the east of the Adriatic

MORAVIAN: see Czech

NORWEGIAN: North Germanic language of Norway

PERSIAN: language of Persia and Iran

POLISH: Slavic language of Poland

PORTUGUESE: Romance language of Portugal and Brazil

ROMANSCH: Rhaeto-Romantic dialects of eastern Switzerland and neighboring parts of Italy

RUMANIAN: Romance language of Rumania

RUSSIAN: Slavic language of Russia

RUTHENIAN: Ukrainian dialect of the Ruthenians

SCOTCH: language of Scotland

SERBIAN: language of southern Slavic people in Serbia and the adjacent republics of Yugoslavia

SLOVAK: language of Slovakia

SLOVENIAN: Slavic language of Slovenia

SPANISH: Romance language of Spain and most of Central America and South America

SWEDISH: North Germanic language of Sweden

SYRIAN: language of Syria

TURKISH: language of Turkey

UKRAINIAN: Slavic language of Ukraine, closely related to Russian

WALLOON: dialect of French spoken by the Walloons, a French-speaking people of Celtic descent inhabiting southern and southeastern Belgium and adjacent regions of France

WELSH: Celtic language of Wales

WENDISH: Slavic language of the Wends (of Saxony and Brandenburg)

WHITE RUSSIAN: East Slavic language of Belarus

YIDDISH: High German language with many words borrowed from Hebrew and Slavic, written in Hebrew characters and spoken chiefly as a vernacular in Eastern European Jewish communities throughout the world

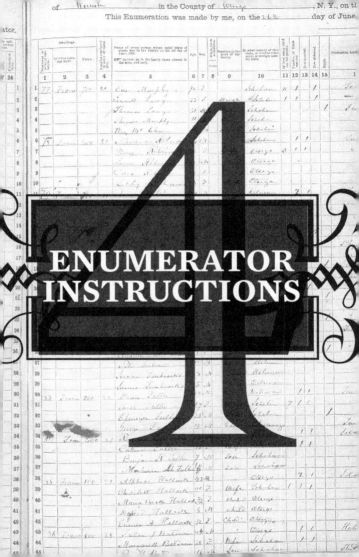

This chapter contains highlights of the instructions given to marshals and enumerators in each federal census from 1790 to 1940.

1790 QUESTIONNAIRE
• Federal government did not provide a uniform printed schedule.

• Marshals submitted returns in whatever form they found convenient.

1800 AND 1810 QUESTIONNAIRES
• Federal government did not provide a uniform printed schedule.

• Some states provided schedules of varying size and typeface.

1820 QUESTIONNAIRE
• Federal government did not provide a uniform printed schedule.

• Some states provided schedules of varying size and typeface.

• All questions were to apply to residents of the household on Aug. 7, 1820, regardless of when the questions were asked.

• Anyone who typically resided at the abode but was absent on Aug. 7, 1820, was still inquired about and marked in the appropriate columns for the abode.

• A person could not be marked as engaging in more than

one occupation (agriculture, commerce, manufacturing). If a person engaged in all three types of work, the enumerator was to mark the occupation that was "the principal and not the occasional, or incidental, occupation of his life."

- Manufacturing was defined as those who work in manufacturing establishments as well as "artificers, handcraftsmen, and mechanics whose labor is preeminently of the hand, and not upon the field."

1830 AND 1840 QUESTIONNAIRES

- Federal government provided a uniform printed schedule.

- Enumerators received a printed list of all questions they were to ask.

- All questions were to apply to residents of the household on June 1 of the census year, regardless of when the questions were asked.

- Anyone who typically resided at the abode but was absent on June 1 was still inquired about and marked in the appropriate columns for the abode.

1850 AND 1860 QUESTIONNAIRES— FREE INHABITANTS

- Federal government provided a uniform printed schedule.

- Enumerators received a printed list of all questions they were to ask.

- All questions were to apply to residents of the household on June 1 of the census year, regardless of when the questions were asked.

- Anyone who typically resided at the abode but was absent on June 1 was still inquired about and marked in the appropriate columns for the abode.

- Each page of the schedule received a heading that contained: the name or number of the district, town or city of the county or parish, and of the state, and the day of the month upon which the enumeration was taken and the signature of the enumerator.

▷ In column 1 (Dwelling Number)

- Tenements were counted as separate houses if they were divided by wooden or brick walls and had separate entrances. Tenements that weren't divided were enumerated as one house.

- If a house was used partly for a store, shop or other purposes, and partly for a dwelling house, it was numbered as a dwelling house.

- Hotels, poorhouses, garrisons, hospitals, asylums, jails, penitentiaries and other similar institutions were numbered as a dwelling house with a description of the house written perpendicularly under the number in said column.

▷ In column 2 (Family Number)

- The term family means "either one person living separately in a house, or a part of a house, and providing for him or herself, or several persons living together in a house, or in part of a house, upon one common means of support, and separately from others in similar circumstances. A widow living alone and separately providing for herself, or 200 individuals living together and provided for by a common head, should each be numbered as one family."

- The resident inmates of a hotel, jail, garrison, hospital, asylum or other similar institution should be reckoned as one family.

▷ In column 3 (Name)
- All landlords, jailors, superintendents of poorhouses, garrisons, hospitals, asylums and other similar institutions, are to be considered as heads of their respective families, and the inmates under their care to be registered as members thereof, and the details concerning each designated in their proper columns.

- Because Indians weren't taxed they were not to be enumerated.

- Students in colleges, academies or schools, when absent from the families to which they belong, were to be enumerated only as members of the family in which they usually boarded and lodged on June 1.

- The sailors and hands of a revenue cutter that belonged to a particular port were to be enumerated as of such port. A similar rule applied to those employed in the navigation of lakes, rivers and canals. All were to be taken at their homes or usual places of abode, whether present or absent; and anyone who lived on board of vessels or boats who were not so enumerated was to be taken as of the place where the vessel or boat was owned, licensed or registered.

▷ In column 4 (Age)
- The age of children under one was stated in fractions, as in one month is one-twelfth.

▷ In column 7 (Profession)
- If a person was a clergyman, enumerators were to insert the initials of his denomination before his profession—Meth. for

Methodist, R.C. for Roman Catholic, O.S.P. for Old School Presbyterian, or other appropriate initials.

▷ **In column 12 (Persons over 20 unable to read and write)**
• If the person could read and write a foreign language, he was considered as able to read and write.

1850 QUESTIONNAIRE— SLAVE INHABITANTS

▷ **Under column 1 (Name of slave owner)**
• If a single slave belonged to several people, the name of only one owner needed to be recorded.

• If a slave was owned by a corporation or trust estate, the name of the trustee or corporation was used in this column.

1870 QUESTIONNAIRE

• Federal government provided a uniform printed schedule.

• Enumerators received a printed list of all questions they were to ask.

• All questions were to apply to residents of the household on June 1, 1870, regardless of when the questions were asked.

• Anyone who typically resided at the abode but was absent on June 1 was still inquired about and marked in the appropriate columns for the abode.

• Each page of the schedule received a heading that contained: the name or number of the district, town or city of the county or parish, and of the state, and the day of the month upon which the enumeration was taken and the signature of the enumerator.

▷ In column 1 (Dwelling number)
• Only a house standing alone, or separated by walls from other houses in a block. was counted as a dwelling house.

• Hotels, poorhouses, garrisons, asylums, jails and similar establishments, where the inmates lived habitually under a single roof, were regarded as single dwelling houses. A description of such establishments was to be written longitudinally in the columns.

• The instructions note that "very many persons, especially in cities, have no other place of abode than stores, shops, etc.; places which are not primarily intended for habitation." These people were to be counted, and the building was to be reckoned as a dwelling house.

▷ In column 2 (Families)
• Family was defined as "one or more persons living together and provided for in common." All the inmates of a boarding house or a hotel were considered a single family, even if there were many husbands with wives and children in residence.

▷ In column 3 (Names)
• Sailors were reported at their land homes, no matter how long they may have been absent.

▷ In column 4 (Age)
• The age of children under one was stated in fractions, as in one month is one-twelfth.

▷ In column 7 (Profession)
• Enumerators were instructed to be as specific as possible:

"Call no man a 'factory hand' or a 'mill operative.' State the kind of a mill or factory. The better form of expression would be, 'works in cotton mill,' 'works in paper mill,' etc. Do not call a man a 'shoemaker,' 'bootmaker,' unless he makes the entire boot or shoe in a small shop. If he works in (or for) a boot and shoe factory, say so."

▷ In column 9 (Personal Estate)

- This figure included the value of all bonds, stocks, mortgages, notes, livestock, jewels or furniture, but didn't include wearing apparel. Personal property valued at less than $100 was not reported.

▷ In column 10 (Place of Birth)

- Enumerators were to be as specific as possible for foreign-born people. Instead of writing "Great Britain" as the place of birth, enumerators were to give the particular country, as England, Scotland or Wales. Instead of "Germany," they were to specify the state, as Prussia, Baden, Bavaria, Wurttemburg, Hesse, Darmstadt, and so on.

▷ In column 18 (Deaf and dumb, Blind, Insane, or Idiotic)

- Enumerators were instructed to try not to give offense with this question. Their instruction included, "The fact of idiocy will be better determined by the common consent of the neighborhood, than by attempting to apply any scientific measure to the weakness of the mind or will."

- Only blindness and undoubted insanity were to be counted in this column.

- Loss of hearing without the loss of speech was not to be reported.

1880 QUESTIONNAIRE
• Federal government provided a uniform printed schedule.

• Enumerators received a printed list of all questions they were to ask.

• All questions were to apply to residents of the household on June 1, 1880, regardless of when the questions were asked.

• Anyone who typically resided at the abode but was absent on June 1 was still inquired about and marked in the appropriate columns for the abode.

• Each page of the schedule received a heading that contained: the name or number of the district, town or city of the county or parish, and of the state, and the day of the month upon which the enumeration was taken and the signature of the enumerator.

• Many of the clarifying instructions from the 1870 census also apply to the 1880 census.

1890 QUESTIONNAIRE
• Federal government provided a uniform printed schedule, and the look was dramatically different, moving to a vertical format.

1900 QUESTIONNAIRE
▷ **In column 3 (Name)**
• Transient guests of a hotel weren't enumerated at the hotel, unless they were likely otherwise to be omitted from the enumeration; but the proprietor and his family, and those

boarders, employees and servants who regularly slept there were to be included.

- Summer boarders at hotels or country houses and persons temporarily residing in foreign lands were enumerated as part of their family at their home or usual place of abode.

- All inmates of hospitals or other institutions were enumerated, and if they had another permanent place of residence, it was to be written in the margin of the schedule on the left-hand side of the page.

- The floating population in vessels, steamboats and houseboats at wharves and piers or river landings was to be enumerated on the morning of June 1, as far as possible, by the enumerators of the districts contiguous to the waterfront, including in the enumeration all persons who claimed to be residents of the United States, even though they had no other home than on board the craft where they were found; but the officers and crew of a foreign ship only temporarily in the harbor were not to be enumerated.

▷ **In columns 11 and 12 (Mother of how many)**
- Stillborn children were not included in these columns.

▷ **In column 13 (Birthplace of this person)**
- If a person was born in what became West Virginia, North Dakota, South Dakota or Oklahoma, it was reported as such, although at the time of his birth, the particular region may have had a different name.

- Only the country was recorded for foreign-born people, with the following exceptions: Ireland, England, Scotland, Wales, Hungary, Bohemia and Finland were distinguished when appropriate.

▷ In column 18 (Naturalized citizen)
- This question applied only to foreign-born males 21 years of age and over.

▷ In column 19 (Occupation)
- If a person had two occupations, the job that supplied the majority of his income was reported.

- A person who received his income, or most of it, from money loaned at interest or from stocks, bonds or other securities, was reported as a "capitalist."

▷ In columns 22 and 23 (Can read and write)
- A person was considered literate if he could read or write in any language.

1910 QUESTIONNAIRE
Many of the instructions for the 1900 census also applied to the 1910 census. Some notable additions include:

▷ In column 4 (Relationship)
- Occupants of an institution or school, living under a common roof, were to be designated as officer, inmate, pupil, patient, prisoner, etc.; and in the case of the chief officer, his title was to be used, as warden, principal, superintendent, etc., instead of the word "Head."

▷ In column 8 (Marital status)
- Persons who were single on April 15 were to be reported as such, even though they may have married between that date and the day of the enumrator's visit; and, similarly, persons who became widowed or divorced after April 15 were to be returned as married if that was their condition on that date.

▷ In column 12 (Birthplace of this person)
• Turkey was distinquished as "Turkey in Europe" and "Turkey in Asia."

▷ In column 17 (Speaks English?)
• See Chapter 3 for a listing of foreign languages used on the census.

▷ In column 20 (Employer or wage earner or working on own account)
• If person kept boarders to supplement his income, he was not listed as a boarding housekeeper. This designation was used only if the boarding house was the person's primary source of income.

• An employer was defined as "one who employs helpers, other than domestic servants, in transacting his own business. The term employer does not include the superintendent, agent, manager, or other person employed to manage an establishment or business; and it does not include the foreman of a room, the boss of a gang, or the coal miner who hires his helper."

• An employee was defined as "any person who works for wages or a salary and is subject to the control and direction of an employer, whether he be president of a large corporation or only a day laborer, whether he be paid in money or in kind, and whether he be employed by his own parent or by another."

• Working on own account was defined as "persons who have a gainful occupation and are neither employers nor employees." Farmers; owners of small establishments who do not employ helpers; professional men who work for fees; and "hucksters, peddlers, newsboys, boot-blacks, etc."were listed as examples of this category.

▷ In column 21 (Out of work 15 April 1910)
- Out of work was limited to persons who wanted work but couldn't find it.

▷ In column 26 (Owned/rented)
- If the family living in the home didn't own the home, either in part or in whole, the family was classified as renting, whether or not they actually paid rent.

▷ In column 31 (Blind)
- People were labeled blind only if they were unable to read even with the help of glasses.

1920 QUESTIONNAIRE
See the instructions for the 1910 census with the exception of these changes:

▷ In column 11 (Age)
- Age for children under 5 years was to be reported in complete years and months.

1930 QUESTIONNAIRE
See the instructions for the 1910 census with the exception of these changes:

▷ In column 5 (Name)
- Cadets at Annapolis and West Point were to be enumerated at the institutions.

- Student nurses were to be counted where they were being trained.

- All other students were counted with their families.

▷ **In column 12 (Color or race)**
• Any mixture of White and some other race was to be reported according to the race of the parent who was not White; mixtures of "colored" races were to be listed according to the father's race.

▷ **In columns 30 and 31 (Veteran)**
• Veteran status excluded persons who served only during peacetime.

1940 QUESTIONNAIRE

Enumerators carried a supply of a separate report form, P-16, which persons who were unwilling to give income information verbally could use. The completed form was to be inserted in an accompanying envelope, sealed and given to the census taker for mailing. Questions 35 through 50 were asked only of a 5 percent sample of the population.

A "household" was defined in terms of "one set of cooking facilities or housekeeping arrangements."

▷ **In column 10 (Color or race)**
• Mexicans were to be listed as White unless they were definitely Indian or some race other than White.

▷ **In columns 39–41 (Veterans)**
• Veteran status was extended to peacetime service as well as during wars and expeditions.

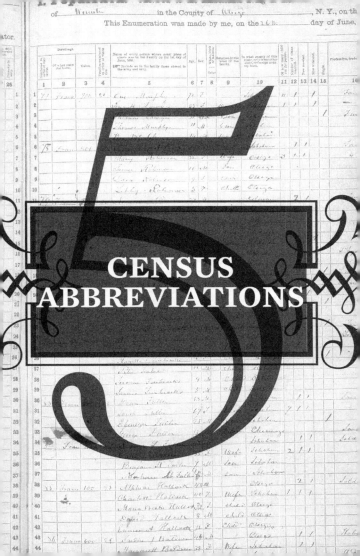

CENSUS ABBREVIATIONS

▷ **Relationships**

A aunt
AD adopted
ADCL adopted child
ADD adopted daughter
ADGCL adopted grandchild
ADM adopted mother
ADS adopted son
AL aunt-in-law
B brother
BBOY bound boy
BGIRL bound girl
BL or **BIL** brother-in-law
BO boarder
C cousin
CAP captain
CHA chamber maid
CIL cousin-in-law
CL child
COM companion
D daughter
DL or **DIL** daughter-in-law
F father
FB foster brother
FF foster father
FIRST C first cousin
FL or **FIL** father-in-law
FM foster mother
FOB foster brother
FOS foster son
FOSI foster sister
G governess
GA great-aunt

GCL grandchild
GD granddaughter
GF grandfather
GGF great-grandfather
GGGF great-great-grandfather
GM grandmother
GGM great-grandmother
GGGM great-great-grandmother
GML grandmother-in-law
GN grand- or great-nephew
GNI grand- or great-niece
GOD CL godchild
GS grandson
GSL grandson-in-law
GU great-uncle
GUA guardian
GUEST guest
H husband
HB half brother
HBL half brother-in-law
HSI half sister
HSIL half sister-in-law
HUSB husband
L lodger
M mother
MAT matron
ML or **MIL** mother-in-law
N nephew
NL nephew-in-law
NI niece
NIL niece-in-law

R roomer
S son
SB stepbrother
SBL stepbrother-in-law
SCL stepchild
SD stepdaughter
SDL stepdaughter-in-law
SE servant
SECL servant's child
SF stepfather
SFL stepfather-in-law
SGD stepgranddaughter
SGS stepgrandson
SI sister
SL son-in-law
SM stepmother
SML stepmother-in-law
SS stepson
SSI stepsister
SSIL stepsister-in-law
SSL stepson-in-law
TEN tenant
U uncle
UL uncle-in-law
VI visitor
W wife
WARD Ward

▷ **Citizenship Status**
AL alien (not naturalized)
PA declaration of intent filed
NA naturalized
NR not recorded

▷ **Color/Ethnicity**
¼ quadroon

⅛ octoroon
B Black
CH Chinese
FIL Filipino
HIN Hindu
I or **IN** American Indian
JP Japanese
KOR Korean
MEX Mexican
M or **MU** Mulatto
NEG Negro
OT Other
W White

▷ **Employment**
E or **EMP** employer
EM self-employed
NP unpaid family worker
O or **OA** own account
W wage or salary worker

▷ **Occupations**
AGRIC agriculture
AGT agent
AP apprentice
ASST assistant
AT attendant
BAR bartender
BU butler
CAP captain
CHA chamber maid
CO company
COA coachman
COMSN commission
COOK cook
DEPT department

DLA day laborer
DOM domestic
DW dishwasher
EMP employee
EN engineer
FAH farm hand
FAL farm laborer
FAW farm worker
FCTY factory
FI fireman
GO governess
HE herder
HELP help
H.GI hired girl
H.H hired hand
HK housekeeper
HM hired man
H.MAID housemaid
HW houseworker
I inmate
INSR insurance
LA laborer
LAU launderer
MAN manager
MERCH merchant
MFG manufacturing
MFR manufacturer
NU nurse
O officer
P patient
PA partner
PH doctor
POR porter
PR prisoner
PREST president
PRI principal

PRV private
PU pupil
R.R. railroad or railway
SA sailor
SAL saleslady
SCH school
SE servant
SECY secretary
SU or **SUPT** superintendent
TELEG telegraph
TELEPH telephone
TRAV traveling or traveler
TREAS treasurer
WA warden
WAI waitress
WKM workman
WT waiter

▷ **Ownership of Home**
F free of mortgage
FM farm
M mortgaged
O owned
R rented

▷ **Military**
UA survivor of the Union Army
UN survivor of the Union Navy
CA survivor of the Confederate Army
CN survivor of the Confederate Navy

▷ War (1930)

BOX Boxer Rebellion
CIV Civil War
MEX Mexican Expedition
PHIL Philippine Insurrection
SP Spanish-American War
WW World War

▷ Deaf, Dumb, Blind, Idiotic

BL blind in both eyes
DD both deaf and dumb

▷ Other Abbreviations

DIST district
DO ditto
DT Dakota Territory
IT Indian Territory
MCD municipal civil district
NR not reported
TWP township

▷ Names

Some of the abbreviations look much different than the full names. In this case, the abbreviations may be based on the Latin forms of the name.

ABIG. Abigail
ABR. Abraham
AGN. Agnes
ALEX. Alexander
ALF. Alfred or Alphonse
AMB. Ambrose

AN. Anne or Anna
AND. Andrew
ANT. Anthony
ART. Arthur
AUG. Augustus
BARB. Barbara
BART. Bartholomew
BENJ. Benjamin
BRID. Bridget
CATH. Catherine
CHAS. Charles
CLEM. Clement
CONST. Constance
CORN. Cornelius
DANL. Daniel
DAV. David
DEB. Deborah
DEN. Dennis
DOUG. Douglas
DY. Dorothy
EDM. Edmund
EDRUS. Edward
EDW. Edward
ELIZ. Elizabeth
ELNR. Eleanor
ESTH. Esther
EZEK. Ezekiel
FRED. Frederick
FS. Francis
GAB. Gabriel
GEO. George
GEOF. Geoffrey
GODF. Godfrey
GREG. Gregory
GUL. William
HAN. Hannah

HEL. Helen
HEN. Henry
HERB. Herbert
HY. Henry
IOH. John
ISB. Isabel
JABUS. James
JAC. James
JAS James
JER. Jeremiah
JNO. John
JON. Jonathan
JOS. Joseph
JOSH. Joshua
JOSH. Josiah
JUD. Judith
LAU. Laurence
LAWR. Lawrence
LEON. Leonard
LYD. Lydia
MARGT. Margaret
MATH. Matthias
MATT. Matthew
MAU. Maurice
MICH. Michael
MICLS. Michael
MILL. Millicent
MY. Mary
NATH. Nathaniel
NICH. Nicholas
NICS. Nicholas
OL. Oliver
PAT. Patrick
PEN. Penelope
PET. Peter

PHIL. Philip
PHIN. Phineas
PHYL. Phyllis
PRISC. Priscilla
PRU. Prudence
RACH. Rachel
RAY. Raymond
REB. Rebecca
REG. Reginald
RIC. Richard
RICHDUS. Richard
ROBT. Robert
ROG. Roger
SAML. Samuel
SAR. Sarah
SILV. Sylvester
SIM. Simon
SOL. Solomon
STE. Stephen
SUS. Susan or Susanna
SUSNA. Susanna
THEO. Theodore
THOS. Thomas
TIM. Timothy
URS. Ursula
VAL.. Valentine
VINC. Vincent
WALT. Walter
WIN. Winifred
WM. William
XPR. Christopher
XTIANUS Christian
XTOPHERUS Christopher
ZACH. Zachariah

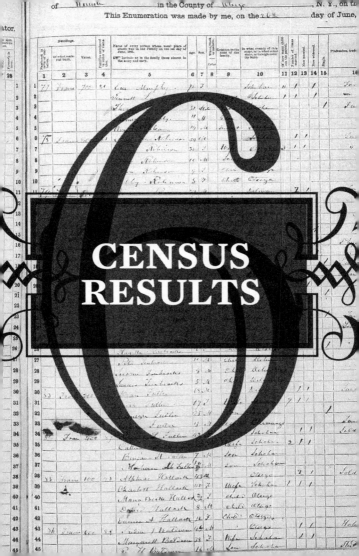

HISTORICAL US POPULATION

1790	3.9 million
1800	5.2 million
1810	7 million
1820	10 million
1830	12.8 million
1840	17 million
1850	23 million
1860	31.4 million
1870	38.6 million
1880	50.2 million
1890	63 million
1900	76.2 million
1910	92.2 million
1920	106 million
1930	123.2 million
1940	132.2 million
1950	151.3 million
1960	179.3 million
1970	203.2 million
1980	226.5 million
1990	248.7 million
2000	281.4 million
2010	308.8 million

MOST COMMON ANCESTRIES IN THE 2000 US CENSUS

ANCESTRY	NUMBER OF PEOPLE	PERCENTAGE OF POPULATION
German	42.8 million	15.2
Irish	30.5 million	10.8
African-American	24.9 million	8.8
English	24.5 million	8.7
American	20.2 million	7.2
Mexican	18.4 million	6.5
Italian	15.6 million	5.6
Polish	9.0 million	3.2
French	8.3 million	3.0
American Indian	7.9 million	2.8
Scottish	4.9 million	1.7
Dutch	4.5 million	1.6
Norwegian	4.5 million	1.6
Scots-Irish	4.3 million	1.5
Swedish	4.0 million	1.4
White	3.8 million	1.4
Puerto Rico	2.7 million	0.9
Russian	2.7 million	0.9
Hispanic	2.5 million	0.9
French Canadian	2.3 million	0.8
Chinese	2.3 million	0.8
Spanish	2.2 million	0.8

Table reflects respondents' self-identified ancestry groups. About 500 ancestries were reported.

FOREIGN-BORN POPULATION

This chart documents the region and country or area of birth for the foreign-born population for the 1980–1950 and 1920–1850 censuses. On the chart, n.e.c. stands for "not elsewhere classified."

REGION AND COUNTRY OR AREA	1980	1970	1960	1950	1920
Total	14,079,906	9,619,302	9,738,091	14,204,149	13,920,692
Reported by region and/or country	13,192,563	9,303,570	9,678,201	14,197,553	13,911,767
Europe	5,149,572	5,740,891	7,256,311	11,784,010	11,916,048
Northern and Western Europe	2,384,257	2,629,200	3,334,971	5,850,256	6,241,916
Northern Europe	1,083,499	1,271,591	1,694,430	3,415,551	3,501,149
British Isles	866,966	937,474	1,171,777	2,147,733	2,172,723
United Kingdom	669,149	686,099	833,055	1,402,923	(NA)
Great Britain	649,318	645,262	764,893	1,224,091	1,135,489
England	442,499	458,114	528,205	809,563	813,853
Scotland	142,001	170,134	213,219	354,323	254,570
Wales	13,528	17,014	23,469	60,205	67,066
Great Britain n.e.c.	51,290	(NA)	(NA)	(NA)	(NA)
Northern Ireland	19,831	40,837	68,162	178,832	(NA)
Ireland	197,817	251,375	338,722	744,810	1,037,234

1910	1900	1890	1880	1870	1860	1850
13,515,886	10,341,276	9,249,547	6,679,943	5,567,229	4,138,697	2,244,602
13,506,272	10,330,534	9,243,535	6,675,875	5,563,637	4,134,809	2,202,625
11,810,115	8,881,548	8,030,347	5,751,823	4,941,049	3,807,062	2,031,867
7,306,325	7,204,649	7,288,917	5,499,889	4,845,679	3,773,347	2,022,195
3,953,947	3,917,815	4,056,160	3,212,431	2,867,926	2,271,661	1,358,887
2,573,534	2,783,082	3,122,911	2,772,169	2,626,241	2,199,079	1,340,812
(NA)	(NA)	(NA)	(NA)	(NA)	(NA)	(NA)
1,221,283	1,167,623	1,251,402	917,598	770,414	587,775	379,093
877,719	840,513	908,141	662,676	550,924	431,692	278,675
261,076	233,524	242,231	170,136	140,835	108,518	70,550
82,488	93,586	100,079	83,302	74,533	45,763	29,868
(NA)	(NA)	951	1,484	4,122	1,802	(NA)
(NA)	(NA)	(NA)	(NA)	(NA)	(NA)	(NA)
1,352,251	1,615,459	1,871,509	1,854,571	1,855,827	1,611,304	961,719

REGION AND COUNTRY OR AREA	1980	1970	1960	1950	1920
Scandinavia	216,533	334,117	522,653	1,267,818	1,328,426
Denmark	42,732	61,410	85,060	179,474	189,154
Finland	29,172	45,499	67,624	142,478	149,824
Iceland	4,156	2,895	2,780	2,764	(NA)
Norway	63,316	97,243	152,698	347,852	363,863
Sweden	77,157	127,070	214,491	595,250	625,585
Western Europe	1,300,758	1,357,609	1,640,541	2,434,705	2,740,767
Low countries	142,748	155,513	173,069	206,375	207,038
Belgium	36,487	41,412	50,294	64,194	62,687
Luxembourg	3,125	3,531	4,360	9,048	12,585
Netherlands	103,136	110,570	118,415	133,133	131,766
Austria	145,607	214,014	304,507	370,914	575,627
France	120,215	105,385	111,582	135,592	153,072
Germany	849,384	832,965	989,815	1,608,814	1,686,108
Switzerland	42,804	49,732	61,568	113,010	118,659
Other Western Europe	(NA)	(NA)	(NA)	(NA)	263

1910	1900	1890	1880	1870	1860	1850
1,380,413	1,134,733	933,249	440,262	241,685	72,582	18,075
181,649	153,690	132,543	64,196	30,107	9,962	1,838
129,680	62,641	(NA)	(NA)	(NA)	(NA)	(NA)
(NA)	(NA)	(NA)	(NA)	(NA)	(NA)	(NA)
403,877	336,388	322,665	181,729	114,246	43,995	12,678
665,207	582,014	478,041	194,337	97,332	18,625	3,559
3,352,378	3,286,834	3,232,757	2,287,458	1,977,753	1,501,686	663,308
172,534	127,719	107,349	86,461	65,157	37,353	11,161
49,400	29,757	22,639	15,535	12,553	9,072	1,313
3,071	3,031	2,882	12,836	5,802	(NA)	(NA)
120,063	94,931	81,828	58,090	46,802	28,281	9,848
626,341	275,907	123,271	38,663	30,508	25,061	946
117,418	104,197	113,174	106,971	116,402	109,870	54,069
2,311,237	2,663,418	2,784,894	1,966,742	1,690,533	1,276,075	583,774
124,848	115,593	104,069	88,621	75,153	53,327	13,358
(NA)	(NA)	(NA)	(NA)	(NA)	(NA)	(NA)

REGION AND COUNTRY OR AREA	1980	1970	1960	1950	1920
Southern and Eastern Europe	2,748,547	3,090,991	3,907,020	5,918,982	5,670,927
Southern Europe	1,336,805	1,363,195	1,541,441	2,133,092	1,939,600
Greece	210,998	177,275	159,167	174,526	175,976
Italy	831,922	1,008,533	1,256,999	1,790,429	1,610,113
Portugal	209,968	119,899	80,276	108,775	103,976
Azores	32,531	28,865	22,586	35,611	33,995
Portugal	177,437	91,034	57,690	73,164	69,981
Spain	73,735	57,488	44,999	59,362	49,535
Other Southern Europe	10,182	(NA)	(NA)	(NA)	(NA)
Eastern Europe	1,411,742	1,727,796	2,365,579	3,785,890	3,731,327
Albania	7,381	9,180	9,618	8,814	5,608
Bulgaria	8,463	8,609	8,223	9,399	10,477
Czechoslovakia	112,707	160,899	227,618	491,638	362,438
Estonia	12,169	12,163	13,991	3,550	(NA)
Hungary	144,368	183,236	245,252	274,450	397,283
Latvia	34,349	41,707	50,681	20,673	(NA)
Lithuania	48,194	76,001	121,475	193,606	135,068
Poland	418,128	548,107	747,750	1,268,583	1,139,979
Romania	66,994	70,687	84,575	146,393	102,823
Soviet Union	406,022	463,462	690,598	1,153,628	1,400,495
Turkey in Europe	(NA)	(NA)	(NA)	2,257	5,284

1910	1900	1890	1880	1870	1860	1850
4,500,932	1,674,648	728,851	248,620	93,824	32,312	9,672
1,544,149	539,968	216,387	66,249	30,416	21,726	8,152
101,282	8,515	1,887	776	390	328	86
1,343,125	484,027	182,580	44,230	17,157	11,677	3,679
77,634	40,376	25,735	15,650	8,973	5,477	1,274
18,274	9,768	9,739	7,512	4,431	1,361	(NA)
59,360	30,608	15,996	8,138	4,542	4,116	1,274
22,108	7,050	6,185	5,121	3,764	4,244	3,113
(NA)	(NA)	(NA)	472	132	(NA)	(NA)
2,956,783	1,134,680	512,464	182,371	63,408	10,586	1,520
(NA)	(NA)	(NA)	(NA)	(NA)	(NA)	(NA)
11,498	(NA)	(NA)	(NA)	(NA)	(NA)	(NA)
219,214	156,891	118,106	85,361	40,289	(NA)	(NA)
(NA)	(NA)	(NA)	(NA)	(NA)	(NA)	(NA)
495,609	145,714	62,435	11,526	3,737	(NA)	(NA)
(NA)	(NA)	(NA)	(NA)	(NA)	(NA)	(NA)
(NA)	(NA)	(NA)	(NA)	(NA)	(NA)	(NA)
937,884	383,407	147,440	48,557	14,436	7,298	(NA)
65,923	15,032	(NA)	(NA)	(NA)	(NA)	(NA)
1,184,412	423,726	182,644	35,722	4,644	3,160	1,414
32,230	9,910	1,839	1,205	302	128	106

REGION AND COUNTRY OR AREA	1980	1970	1960	1950	1920	
Yugoslavia	152,967	153,745	165,798	211,416	169,439	
Other Eastern Europe	(NA)	(NA)	(NA)	1,483	2,433	
Europe n.e.c.	16,768	20,700	14,320	14,772	3,205	
Asia	2,539,777	824,887	490,996	275,665	237,950	
Armenia	(NA)	(NA)	(NA)	32,166	36,628	
China	286,120	172,132	99,735	46,129	43,560	
India	206,087	51,000	12,296	5,850	4,901	
Japan	221,794	120,235	109,175	70,993	81,502	
Palestine	(NA)	(NA)	(NA)	6,137	3,203	
Syria	22,081	14,962	16,717	57,227	51,901	
Turkey in Asia	51,915	48,085	52,228	46,654	11,019	
Other Asia	1,751,780	418,473	200,845	10,509	5,236	
Africa	199,723	80,143	35,355	18,326	16,126	
Africa excl. Atlantic Islands	189,266	61,463	27,053	8,859	5,781	
Atlantic Islands	10,457	18,680	8,302	9,467	10,345	
Oceania	77,577	41,258	34,730	17,343	14,626	
Australia	36,120	24,271	22,209	12,816	10,914	
Sandwich Islands (Hawaii)	(NA)	(NA)	(NA)	(NA)	(NA)	
Other Oceania	41,457	16,987	12,521	4,527	3,712	

1910	1900	1890	1880	1870	1860	1850
(NA)	(NA)	(NA)	(NA)	(NA)	(NA)	(NA)
10,013	(NA)	(NA)	(NA)	(NA)	(NA)	(NA)
2,858	2,251	12,579	3,314	1,546	1,403	(NA)
191,484	120,248	113,383	107,630	64,565	36,796	1,135
(NA)	(NA)	(NA)	(NA)	(NA)	(NA)	(NA)
56,756	81,534	106,688	104,468	63,042	35,565	758
4,664	2,031	2,143	1,707	586	(NA)	(NA)
67,744	24,788	2,292	401	73	(NA)	(NA)
(NA)	(NA)	(NA)	(NA)	(NA)	(NA)	(NA)
(NA)	(NA)	(NA)	(NA)	(NA)	(NA)	(NA)
59,729	(NA)	(NA)	(NA)	(NA)	(NA)	(NA)
2,591	11,895	2,260	1,054	864	1,231	377
3,992	2,538	2,207	2,204	2,657	526	551
3,992	2,538	2,207	2,204	2,657	526	551
(NA)	(NA)	(NA)	(NA)	(NA)	(NA)	(NA)
11,450	8,820	9,353	6,859	4,028	2,140	588
9,035	6,807	5,984	4,906	3,118	1,419	(NA)
(NA)	(NA)	1,304	1,147	584	435	588
2,415	2,013	2,065	806	326	286	(NA)

REGION OR COUNTRY AND AREA	1980	1970	1960	1950	1920
Latin America	4,372,487	1,803,970	908,309	791,840	588,843
Caribbean	1,258,363	675,108	193,922	106,241	78,962
Cuba	607,814	439,048	79,150	18,493	14,872
Other Caribbean	650,549	236,060	114,772	87,748	64,090
Central America	2,553,113	873,624	624,851	651,976	491,330
Mexico	2,199,221	759,711	575,902	641,462	486,418
Other Central America	353,892	113,913	48,949	10,514	4,912
South America	561,011	255,238	89,536	33,623	18,551
Northern America	853,427	812,421	952,500	1,310,369	1,138,174
Canada	842,859	812,421	952,500	1,310,369	1,138,174
Canada-French	(NA)	(NA)	(NA)	370,852	307,786
Canada-Other	(NA)	(NA)	(NA)	915,537	817,139
Newfoundland	(NA)	(NA)	(NA)	23,980	13,249
Other Northern America	10,568	(NA)	(NA)	(NA)	(NA)
Region or country not reported	887,343	315,732	59,890	6,596	8,925
Born at sea	(NA)	(NA)	(NA)	5,008	5,336
Not reported	(NA)	(NA)	(NA)	1,588	3,589

1910	1900	1890	1880	1870	1860	1850
279,514	137,458	107,307	90,073	57,871	38,315	20,773
47,635	25,435	23,256	16,401	11,570	7,353	5,772
15,133	11,081	(NA)	6,917	5,319	(NA)	(NA)
32,502	14,354	(NA)	9,484	6,251	(NA)	(NA)
223,651	107,290	79,045	69,106	42,736	27,699	13,458
221,915	103,393	77,853	68,399	42,435	27,466	13,317
1,736	3,897	1,192	707	301	233	141
8,228	4,733	5,006	4,566	3,565	3,263	1,543
1,209,717	1,179,922	980,938	717,286	493,467	249,970	147,711
1,209,717	1,179,922	980,938	717,157	493,464	249,970	147,711
385,083	395,126	302,496	(NA)	(NA)	(NA)	(NA)
819,554	784,796	678,442	(NA)	(NA)	(NA)	(NA)
5,080	(NA)	(NA)	(NA)	(NA)	(NA)	(NA)
(NA)	(NA)	(NA)	129	3	(NA)	(NA)
9,614	10,742	6,012	4,068	3,592	3,888	41,977
6,927	8,196	5,533	4,068	2,638	2,522	(NA)
2,687	2,546	479	(NA)	954	1,366	41,977

YEAR	TOTAL POPULATION	NATIVE POPULATION					FOREIGN-BORN POPULATION
		TOTAL	BORN IN THE UNITED STATES	BORN ABROAD			
				TOTAL	IN OUTLYING AREAS	OF AMERICAN PARENTS	
1990	248,709,873	228,942,557	225,695,826	3,246,731	1,382,446	1,864,285	19,767,316
1980	226,545,805	212,465,899	210,322,697	2,143,202	1,088,172	1,055,030	14,079,906
1970	203,210,158	193,590,856	191,329,489	2,261,367	891,266	1,370,101	9,619,302
1960	179,325,671	169,587,580	168,525,645	1,061,935	660,425	401,510	9,738,091
1950	150,216,110	139,868,715	139,442,390	426,325	329,970	96,355	10,347,395
1940	131,669,275	120,074,379	119,795,254	279,125	156,956	122,169	11,594,896
1930	122,775,046	108,570,897	108,304,188	266,709	136,032	130,677	14,204,149
1920	105,710,620	91,789,928	91,659,045	130,883	38,020	92,863	13,920,692
1910	91,972,266	78,456,380	78,381,104	75,276	7,365	67,911	13,515,886
1900	75,994,575	65,653,299	65,583,225	70,074	2,923	67,151	10,341,276
1890	62,622,250	53,372,703	53,362,371	10,332	322	10,010	9,249,547
1880	50,155,783	43,475,840	43,475,498	342	51	291	6,679,943
1870	38,558,371	32,991,142	32,990,922	220	51	169	5,567,229
1860	31,443,321	27,304,624	27,304,624	-	-	-	4,138,697
1850	23,191,876	20,947,274	20,947,274	-	-	-	2,244,602

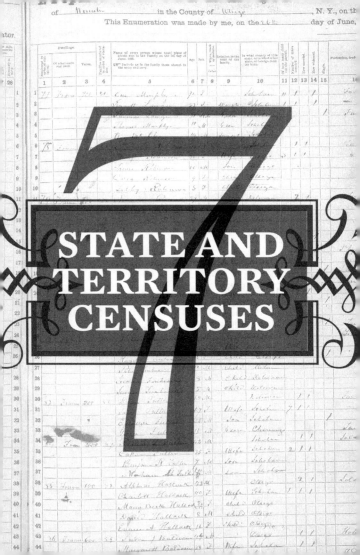

7
STATE AND TERRITORY CENSUSES

ALABAMA
FIRST FEDERAL CENSUS: 1830

COLONIAL, TERRITORIAL AND STATE CENSUSES: 1706–1819 (various years); 1820 (eight counties); 1850, 1855, 1866, 1907 (Confederate veterans); 1921 (Confederate pensioners)

ALASKA
FIRST FEDERAL CENSUS: 1900

COLONIAL, TERRITORIAL AND STATE CENSUSES: 1878 (Aleutian Islands); 1879, 1881 (Sitka); 1885 (Cape Smith, Point Barrow); 1890–1895 (Pribiloff Islands); 1904–1907, 1914, 1917 (St. Paul and St. George islands); 1890 (Naval Veterans)

ARIZONA
FIRST FEDERAL CENSUS: 1870

COLONIAL, TERRITORIAL AND STATE CENSUSES: 1801, 1852 (Pimeria Alta); 1831 (Santa Cruz County); 1860; 1864; 1866; 1882 (several counties); 1883 (Pensioners on the Roll)

ARKANSAS
FIRST FEDERAL CENSUS: 1830

COLONIAL, TERRITORIAL AND STATE CENSUSES: 1686–1804, 1823, 1829 (fragments)

CALIFORNIA
FIRST FEDERAL CENSUS: 1850

COLONIAL, TERRITORIAL AND STATE CENSUSES: 1793, 1796, 1797, 1798 (various areas); 1834 (Santa Barbara); 1852; 1870 (San Francisco County)

COLORADO
FIRST FEDERAL CENSUS: 1860 (as four territories), 1870 (as Colorado Territory), 1880 (as a state)

COLONIAL, TERRITORIAL AND STATE CENSUSES: 1861, 1866 (fragments), 1885; 1898 (Volunteers for the Spanish American War); 1904-1908 (Ute Census of Navajo Springs)

CONNECTICUT
FIRST FEDERAL CENSUS: 1790

COLONIAL, TERRITORIAL AND STATE CENSUSES: 1917 (males of military service age, some women)

DELAWARE
FIRST FEDERAL CENSUS: 1800

COLONIAL, TERRITORIAL AND STATE CENSUSES: 1671, 1782

DISTRICT OF COLUMBIA
FIRST FEDERAL CENSUS: 1800

COLONIAL, TERRITORIAL AND STATE CENSUSES: none known (see listings for Maryland and Virginia)

FLORIDA
FIRST FEDERAL CENSUS: 1830

COLONIAL, TERRITORIAL AND STATE CENSUSES: 1783; 1784–1786; 1790; 1793; 1813; 1814; 1815; 1820 (Pensacola and Escambia River Areas); 1824 (fragments); 1825 (Leon County); 1837; 1840 (military); 1845; 1855 (Marion County); 1867 (several counties); 1875 (Alachua County); 1885; 1895 (Nassau County); 1945

GEORGIA
FIRST FEDERAL CENSUS: 1820

COLONIAL, TERRITORIAL AND STATE CENSUSES: 1787–1866 (various years; fragments survive); 1835 (military pensioners); 1864 (Census for Re-organizing the Georgia Militia)

HAWAII
FIRST FEDERAL CENSUS: 1900

COLONIAL, TERRITORIAL AND STATE CENSUSES: 1847 (foreigners); 1866; 1878 (Hawaii, Maui, Oahu); 1890; 1896 (Honolulu)

IDAHO
FIRST FEDERAL CENSUS: 1850 (as Oregon Territory)

COLONIAL, TERRITORIAL AND STATE CENSUSES: none known

ILLINOIS
FIRST FEDERAL CENSUS: 1820

COLONIAL, TERRITORIAL AND STATE CENSUSES: 1810 (Randolph County, as Indiana Territory); 1818; 1820–1845 (every five years, various counties); 1855; 1865; 1880 (Cook County)

INDIANA
FIRST FEDERAL CENSUS: 1820

COLONIAL, TERRITORIAL AND STATE CENSUSES: 1807; 1816 (postmasters); 1820-on (various years, males older than 21); 1880 (Clark County)

IOWA
FIRST FEDERAL CENSUS: 1850

COLONIAL, TERRITORIAL AND STATE CENSUSES: 1836 (in Wisconsin Territory); 1838–1897 (various years and communities); 1851; 1852; 1856; 1885; 1895; 1905; 1915; 1925

KANSAS
FIRST FEDERAL CENSUS: 1860

COLONIAL, TERRITORIAL AND STATE CENSUSES: 1857 (Shawnee tribe); 1865–1925 (every 10 years); 1873-on (various years and areas); 1855, 1856, 1857, 1858, 1859, 1883 (pensioners);

1941 (veterinarians); 1878–1894 (Institution for the Education of the Blind)

KENTUCKY
FIRST FEDERAL CENSUS: 1810

COLONIAL, TERRITORIAL AND STATE CENSUSES: 1859 (lawyers)

LOUISIANA
FIRST FEDERAL CENSUS: 1810

COLONIAL, TERRITORIAL AND STATE CENSUSES: 1699, 1700, 1706, 1711, 1721, 1722, 1724, 1725, 1726, 1727, 1731, 1732, 1766, 1771, 1772, 1774, 1782, 1784–1786, 1788–1790, 1795, 1798, 1799, 1803, 1805 (various communities); 1792–1806, 1809 (Nacogdoches); 1791 (New Orleans); 1812–1815 (War of 1812 pensioners); 1911 (Confederate soldiers and widows)

MAINE
FIRST FEDERAL CENSUS: 1790

COLONIAL, TERRITORIAL AND STATE CENSUSES: 1837 (Bangor, Portland, unincorporated towns)

MARYLAND
FIRST FEDERAL CENSUS: 1790

COLONIAL, TERRITORIAL AND STATE CENSUSES: 1776, 1778

MASSACHUSETTS
FIRST FEDERAL CENSUS: 1790

COLONIAL, TERRITORIAL AND STATE CENSUSES: 1855, 1865

MICHIGAN
FIRST FEDERAL CENSUS: 1820

COLONIAL, TERRITORIAL AND STATE CENSUSES: 1710, various through 1792 (Detroit area); 1780 (Fort St. Joseph); 1796 (Wayne County); 1827, 1837 (Kalamazoo County); 1845, 1854-1894 (every 10 years); 1883 (pensioners); 1894 (veterans)

MINNESOTA
FIRST FEDERAL CENSUS: 1820 (in Michigan Territory)

COLONIAL, TERRITORIAL AND STATE CENSUSES: 1836 (in Wisconsin Territory); 1849; 1850; 1853 (various areas); 1855 (fragments); 1857, 1865, 1875, 1885, 1895, 1905

MISSISSIPPI
FIRST FEDERAL CENSUS: 1820

COLONIAL, TERRITORIAL AND STATE CENSUSES: 1792 (Natchez); 1784, 1787, 1788, 1794, 1798–1817 (various years); 1831 (Choctaw tribe); 1822–1825, 1837, 1841, 1845, 1853, 1866 (various areas); 1790 (Tobacco growers in the Spanish Natchez district); 1792, 1805, 1810, 1813, 1815–1818, 1820, 1830, 1850, 1860

MISSOURI
FIRST FEDERAL CENSUS: 1830

COLONIAL, TERRITORIAL AND STATE CENSUSES: 1770–1804 (various areas); 1797, 1803 (New Madrid); 1817, 1819 (St.

Charles); 1840, 1844, 1852, 1856, 1857–1858, 1868–1869, 1873, 1876 (fragments); 1880, 1881

MONTANA
FIRST FEDERAL CENSUS: 1870

COLONIAL, TERRITORIAL AND STATE CENSUSES: 1883 (pensioners); 1897–1898 (Blackfeet tribe)

NEBRASKA
FIRST FEDERAL CENSUS: 1860

COLONIAL, TERRITORIAL AND STATE CENSUSES: 1854, 1855, 1856, 1860, 1865, 1869, 1885; 1893 (veterans)

NEVADA
FIRST FEDERAL CENSUS: 1850

COLONIAL, TERRITORIAL AND STATE CENSUSES: 1776, 1862, 1863, 1875

NEW HAMPSHIRE
FIRST FEDERAL CENSUS: 1790

COLONIAL, TERRITORIAL AND STATE CENSUSES: 1732, 1744, 1767, 1776

NEW JERSEY
FIRST FEDERAL CENSUS: 1830 (Cumberland County only in 1800)

COLONIAL, TERRITORIAL AND STATE CENSUSES: 1824–1832 (Paterson); 1855, 1865, 1875, 1885, 1895, 1905, 1915

NEW MEXICO
FIRST FEDERAL CENSUS: 1850

COLONIAL, TERRITORIAL AND STATE CENSUSES: 1600; 1750–1845 (various years and areas); 1790, 1788 and 1790 (El Paso del Norte); 1864, 1885

NEW YORK
FIRST FEDERAL CENSUS: 1790

COLONIAL, TERRITORIAL AND STATE CENSUSES: 1693; 1700 (militia); 1774–1776, 1825–1875 (every 10 years); 1892, 1905, 1915, 1925

NORTH CAROLINA
FIRST FEDERAL CENSUS: 1790

COLONIAL, TERRITORIAL AND STATE CENSUSES: 1784–1787; 1838 (Indian removal); 1793–1840 (Black craftsmen); 1852 (pensioners)

NORTH DAKOTA
FIRST FEDERAL CENSUS: 1900

COLONIAL, TERRITORIAL AND STATE CENSUSES: 1857 (Pembina County); 1885–1939 (various Indian reservations); 1855, 1915, 1925

OHIO
FIRST FEDERAL CENSUS: 1820 (Washington County only in 1800 and 1810)

COLONIAL, TERRITORIAL AND STATE CENSUSES: 1863 (African-American residents arriving between 1861 and 1863)

OKLAHOMA
FIRST FEDERAL CENSUS: 1860

COLONIAL, TERRITORIAL AND STATE CENSUSES: 1880, 1890, 1896 (Cherokee tribe); 1890; 1907 (Seminole County)

OREGON
FIRST FEDERAL CENSUS: 1850

COLONIAL, TERRITORIAL AND STATE CENSUSES: 1842, 1843, 1845, 1846, 1849; 1853–1859 (every year); 1865–1905 (every 10 years)

PENNSYLVANIA
FIRST FEDERAL CENSUS: 1790

COLONIAL, TERRITORIAL AND STATE CENSUSES: 1680 (residents along the Delaware River); 1902 (children in soldier's orphan schools)

RHODE ISLAND
FIRST FEDERAL CENSUS: 1790

COLONIAL, TERRITORIAL AND STATE CENSUSES: 1730 (fragments); 1740–1743, 1747, 1774, 1777 (men age 16 and older); 1782 (partial); 1865, 1875, 1885, 1905, 1915, 1925, 1935

SOUTH CAROLINA
FIRST FEDERAL CENSUS: 1790

COLONIAL, TERRITORIAL AND STATE CENSUSES: 1770 (Tryon County); 1779 (96th district); 1781 (unknown counties); 1829 (Fairfield and Laurens districts); 1839 (Kershaw and Chesterfield districts); 1868, 1869, 1875 (several counties)

SOUTH DAKOTA
FIRST FEDERAL CENSUS: 1900

COLONIAL, TERRITORIAL AND STATE CENSUSES: 1836 (in Wisconsin Territory); 1840 (in Iowa Territory); 1850 (Minnesota Territory); 1860, 1870, 1880 (Dakota Territory); 1885–1945 (every 10 years); 1885–1940 (Indian census, various years)

TENNESSEE
FIRST FEDERAL CENSUS: 1830 (fragments for 1810; 26 counties only for 1820)

COLONIAL, TERRITORIAL AND STATE CENSUSES: 1770–1790 (Cumberland settlements)

TEXAS
FIRST FEDERAL CENSUS: 1850

COLONIAL, TERRITORIAL AND STATE CENSUSES: 1783–1836 (various years and areas), 1828

UTAH
FIRST FEDERAL CENSUS: 1850 (actually taken in 1851)

COLONIAL, TERRITORIAL AND STATE CENSUSES: 1852, 1856, 1872, 1896

VERMONT
FIRST FEDERAL CENSUS: 1790

COLONIAL, TERRITORIAL AND STATE CENSUSES: 1785

VIRGINIA
FIRST FEDERAL CENSUS: 1810 (partial)

COLONIAL, TERRITORIAL AND STATE CENSUSES: 1624, 1625, 1782–1786, 1890 (Union veterans census of southwest Virginia)

WASHINGTON
FIRST FEDERAL CENSUS: 1860

COLONIAL, TERRITORIAL AND STATE CENSUSES: 1857–1892 (various years and areas)

WEST VIRGINIA
FIRST FEDERAL CENSUS: 1870 (earlier censuses as part of Virginia)

COLONIAL, TERRITORIAL AND STATE CENSUSES: see Virginia state censuses

WISCONSIN
FIRST FEDERAL CENSUS: 1820

COLONIAL, TERRITORIAL AND STATE CENSUSES: 1836–1847 (various years and counties); 1855, 1865 (fragments); 1875–1905 (every 10 years)

WYOMING
FIRST FEDERAL CENSUS: 1870

COLONIAL, TERRITORIAL AND STATE CENSUSES: 1855–1905 (every 10 years); 1869; 1878 (Cheyenne)

US TERRITORIES

AMERICAN SAMOA
US FEDERAL CENSUS: 1900 (Armed Forces—Foreign Countries), 1910, 1920, 1930

CUBA
US FEDERAL CENSUS: 1900 (Armed Forces—Foreign Countries)

GUAM
US FEDERAL CENSUS: 1900 (Armed Forces—Foreign Countries), 1910, 1920, 1930

PANAMA CANAL ZONE
US FEDERAL CENSUS: 1910, 1920, 1930

PHILIPPINES
SPANISH RECORDS begin in late 1500s; various records from 1800–1898 (Luzon and Central Visayas)

US FEDERAL CENSUS: 1900 (Armed Forces—Foreign Countries), 1910, 1920

PUERTO RICO
US FEDERAL CENSUS: 1900 (Armed Forces—Foreign Countries), 1910, 1920, 1930

US VIRGIN ISLANDS
US FEDERAL CENSUS: 1920, 1930

SPECIAL SCHEDULES

There's more to the census than those every-10-years counts. The government took special censuses (also called nonpopulation censuses) to count unique segments of the population or create snapshots of communities. Taken variously during and between regular census years, these enumerations counted farms, veterans, factories, American Indians and other groups.

Not all of these schedules survived, and many aren't yet available online. But if your ancestors are listed, you can learn things you might not find in any other record. These special censuses of select populations may have just the ancestor answers you need.

SCHEDULE OF DEFECTIVE, DEPENDENT AND DELINQUENT CLASSES

YEARS: 1880

HOW TO KNOW IF YOUR ANCESTOR IS LISTED: Find him in the regular 1880 population census, looking carefully for marks in columns 15 through 20, showing whether the person is sick or temporarily disabled; blind; deaf and dumb; idiotic; insane; or maimed, crippled, bedridden or otherwise disabled.

WHERE TO FIND IT: The Family History Library <familysearch.org> and the National Archives <nara.org> have some of this schedule on microfilm, but most of these records are housed in state repositories, listed below:

▷ **Alabama**
Alabama Department of Archives & History, Montgomery
<www.archives.state.al.us>

▷ **Arkansas**
Arkansas History Commission, Little Rock

<www.ark-ives.com/research/materials/census_records.asp>
St. Louis County Library, St. Louis <www.slcl.org/genealogy-and-local-history/finding-aids-and-guides>

▷ **California**
California State Library, Sacramento <www.library.ca.gov>

▷ **Colorado**
Duke University, Durham, NC
<library.duke.edu/research/subject/guides/us-census>

▷ **Connecticut**
Connecticut State Library, Hartford
<www.cslib.org/speccens.htm>

▷ **Dakota Territory**
South Dakota State Archives, Pierre
<http://www.statearchives.us/south-dakota.htm>

▷ **Delaware**
Delaware Public Archives Hall of Records, Dover
<archives.delaware.gov>

Family History Library (FHL) microfilm 1421306
<www.familysearch.org>

▷ **District of Columbia**
Allen County Public Library Genealogy Center, Fort Wayne, Ind. <www.genealogycenter.org>

Duke University, Durham, NC
<library.duke.edu/research/subject/guides/us-census>

Mid-Continent Public Library Midwest Genealogy Center, Independence, Mo. <www.mymcpl.org/genealogy>

National Archives & Records Administration (NARA) microfilm M1795 **<archives.gov>**

▷ **Florida**
State Archives of Florida, Tallahassee **<dlis.dos.state.fl.us>**

▷ **Georgia**
Allen County Public Library Genealogy Center, Fort Wayne, Ind. **<www.genealogycenter.org>**

Duke University, Durham, NC **<library.duke.edu/research/subject/guides/us-census>**

Mid-Continent Public Library Midwest Genealogy Center, Independence, Mo. **<www.mymcpl.org/genealogy>**

NARA microfilm T1137 **<archives.gov>**

▷ **Idaho**
Idaho State Historical Society, Boise **<history.idaho.gov>**

▷ **Illinois**
Illinois State Archives, Springfield **<www.sos.state.il.us/departments/archives/research_series/rseries4.html>**

▷ **Indiana**
Indiana State Archives, Indianapolis **<www.in.gov/icpr/3016.htm>**

▷ **Iowa**
Allen County Public Library Genealogy Center, Fort Wayne, Ind. **<www.genealogycenter.org>**

Burlington Public Library, Burlington **<www.burlington.lib.ia.us/genealogy/census.html>**

Mid-Continent Public Library Midwest Genealogy Center, Independence, Mo. **<www.mymcpl.org/genealogy>**

State Historical Society of Iowa, Des Moines
<www.iowahistory.org/libraries>

▷ **Kansas**
FHL microfilms 1602473–1602476 **<www.familysearch.org>**

Kansas State Historical Society, Topeka
**<www.kshs.org/genealogists/census/kansas/
census1880ks.htm#special>**

Mid-Continent Public Library Midwest Genealogy Center, Independence, Mo. **<www.mymcpl.org/genealogy>**

NARA microfilm T1130 **<archives.gov>**

▷ **Kentucky**
Duke University, Durham, NC
<library.duke.edu/research/subject/guides/us-census>

Kentucky Department for Libraries & Archives, Frankfort
<www.kdla.ky.gov/collections.htm>

Mid-Continent Public Library Midwest Genealogy Center, Independence, Mo. **<www.mymcpl.org/genealogy>**

NARA film M1528 **<archives.gov>**

▷ **Louisiana**
Allen County Public Library Genealogy Center, Fort Wayne, Ind. **<www.genealogycenter.org>**

Duke University, Durham, NC
<library.duke.edu/research/subject/guides/us-census>
FHL film 1549554 <www.familysearch.org>

Louisiana State University Library, Baton Rouge
<www.lib.lsu.edul>

Mid-Continent Public Library Midwest Genealogy Center,
Independence, Mo. <www.mymcpl.org/genealogy>

NARA microfilm T1136 <archives.gov>

St. Louis County Library, St Louis <www.slcl.org/genealogy-
and-local-history/finding-aids-and-guides>

▷ **Maine**
Maine State Archives, Augusta
<www.mainehistory.org/gen_howto.shtml>

▷ **Massachusetts**
Allen County Public Library Genealogy Center, Fort Wayne,
Ind. <www.genealogycenter.org>

Massachusetts State Archives, Boston
<www.sec.state.ma.us/arc/arccol/colidx.htm>

Mid-Continent Public Library Midwest Genealogy Center,
Independence, Mo. <www.mymcpl.org/genealogy>

NARA film T1204 <archives.gov>

▷ **Mississippi**
St. Louis County Library, St. Louis <www.slcl.org/genealogy-
and-local-history/finding-aids-and-guides>

Mississippi Department of Archives and History, Jackson
<mdah.state.ms.us>

▷ **Missouri**
Missouri History Museum, Library & Research Center,
St. Louis <www.mohistory.org/lrc-home>

St. Louis County Library, St. Louis <www.slcl.org/genealogy-
and-local-history/finding-aids-and-guides>

State Historical Society of Missouri, Columbia
<shs.umsystem.edu/research/guides/census.shtml>

▷ **Montana**
FHL film 2155438 <www.familysearch.org>

Mid-Continent Public Library Midwest Genealogy Center,
Independence, Mo. <www.mymcpl.org/genealogy>

Montana Historical Society, Helena
<montanahistoricalsociety.org/research>

NARA microfilm M1806 <archives.gov>

▷ **Nebraska**
Allen County Public Library Genealogy Center, Fort Wayne,
Ind. <www.genealogycenter.org>

FHL film 1025186 <www.familysearch.org>

Mid-Continent Public Library Midwest Genealogy Center, Independence, Mo. <www.mymcpl.org/genealogy>

NARA microfilm T1128 <archives.gov>

Nebraska State Historical Society, Lincoln
<www.nebraskahistory.org>

▷ **Nevada**
Nevada State Library and Archives, Reno
<nsla.nevadaculture.org>

▷ **New Hampshire**
New Hampshire State Library, Concord <www.nh.gov/nhsl>

▷ **New Jersey**
New Jersey Division of Archives and Records Management,
Trenton <www.state.nj.us/state/darm/links/guides/
fce00007.html>

▷ **New York**
New York Public Library, New York City
<www.nypl.org/locations/tid/36/node/107590>

New York State Library, Albany
<www.nysl.nysed.gov/genealogy/fedcen.htm>

▷ **North Carolina**
North Carolina State Archives
<www.archives.ncdcr.gov/default.htm>

▷ **Ohio**
Allen County Public Library Genealogy Center, Fort Wayne,
Ind. <www.genealogycenter.org>

FHL films 1602423 and 1602424 <www.familysearch.org>

Mid-Continent Public Library Midwest Genealogy Center,
Independence, Mo. <www.mymcpl.org/genealogy>

NARA microfilm T1159 <archives.gov>

Ohio Historical Society (Fulton through Medina counties, roll T1159), Columbus <www.ohiohistory.org/resource/archlib>

State Library of Ohio, Columbus <library.ohio.gov>

▷ **Pennsylvania**
State Library of Pennsylvania, Harrisburg
<www.portal.state.pa.us/portal/server.pt/community/
genealogy_and_local_history/8730>

Mid-Continent Public Library Midwest Genealogy Center, Independence, Mo. <www.mymcpl.org/genealogy>

NARA microfilm M597 <archives.gov>

▷ **South Carolina**
FHL film 1294286 <www.familysearch.org>

South Carolina Department of Archives & History, Columbia <archives.sc.gov>

▷ **Tennessee**
Allen County Public Library Genealogy Center, Fort Wayne, Ind. <www.genealogycenter.org>

Duke University, Durham, NC
<library.duke.edu/research/subject/guides/us-census>

FHL films 1549481 and 1549482 <www.familysearch.org>

Mid-Continent Public Library Midwest Genealogy Center, Independence, Mo. <www.mymcpl.org/genealogy>

NARA microfilm T1135 <archives.gov>

▷ **Texas**
Allen County Public Library Genealogy Center, Fort Wayne, Ind. **<www.genealogycenter.org>**

FHL film 1421043 **<www.familysearch.org>**

Mid-Continent Public Library Midwest Genealogy Center, Independence, Mo. **<www.mymcpl.org/genealogy>**

NARA film T1134 **<archives.gov>**

Texas State Library and Archvies, Austin
<www.tsl.state.tx.us>

University of North Texas, Denton (except one roll)
<www.library.unt.edu>

▷ **Utah**
FHL film 1550325 **<www.familysearch.org>**

▷ **Virginia**
Allen County Public Library Genealogy Center, Fort Wayne, Ind. **<www.genealogycenter.org>**

Library of Virginia, Richmond **<www.lva.virginia.gov>**

Mid-Continent Public Library Midwest Genealogy Center, Independence, Mo. **<www.mymcpl.org/genealogy>**

NARA film T1132 **<archives.gov>**

▷ **Washington Territory**
FHL film 1549443 **<www.familysearch.org>**

Mid-Continent Public Library Midwest Genealogy Center, Independence, Mo. **<www.mymcpl.org/genealogy>**
NARA microfilm A1154 **<archives.gov>**

Washington State Library
<www.secstate.wa.gov/library/genealogy.aspx>

▷ **West Virginia**
West Virginia Division of Culture and History, Charleston
<www.wvculture.org>

▷ **Wisconsin**
Wisconsin Historical Society, Madison
<www.wisconsinhistory.org/genealogy>

▷ **Tips and tricks**
• Separate schedules list the indigent, blind, deaf and dumb, and other designations.

• You might be surprised to find a relative in this enumeration. What we know today as postpartum depression and menopause could get women of the past temporarily or permanently committed.

AGRICULTURAL CENSUSES

YEARS: 1820, 1850, 1860, 1870, 1880

HOW TO KNOW IF YOUR ANCESTOR IS LISTED: Industry schedules were completed for someone denoted as a business owner in the 1820, 1850, 1860, 1870 and 1880 censuses, whose business had an annual gross product of $500 or more.

WHERE TO FIND IT: The 1820 schedules are on 27 rolls of microfilm in NARA's record group 29, arranged alphabetically by county within each state. Each roll contains an index. Manufacturing/industry schedules for 1850 through 1880 are microfilmed with agricultural censuses for those years.

▷ **Tips and tricks**
• These schedules enumerated manufacturing, mining, fisheries, mercantile, commercial and trading business.

• Information collected generally includes the name of the company or owner, the kind of business, capital invested, and the quantity and value of materials, labor, machinery and products.

SLAVE SCHEDULES

YEARS: 1850 and 1860

HOW TO KNOW IF YOUR ANCESTOR IS LISTED: All slaves were noted demographically under the owner's name; no slave names were listed.

WHERE TO FIND IT: Slave schedules are online at Ancestry.com **<ancestry.com>**, or you can view them on microfilm at the FHL, FHCs and NARA. All available 1850 slave schedules are indexed on FamilySearch.org **<familysearch.org>**.

▷ **Tips and tricks**
• Find former slave ancestors in the 1870 census by subtracting 10 years from your subjects' 1870 ages to estimate their ages in 1860, and compare the ages of your ancestor's family group in 1860 with slaves' ages in households in the slave schedule.

MORTALITY SCHEDULES

YEARS: 1850, 1860, 1870, 1880, 1885 (some areas), 1900 (Minnesota only)

HOW TO KNOW IF YOUR ANCESTOR IS LISTED: Enumerators recorded the names of people who died during the 12-month period prior to the official census date.

WHERE TO FIND IT: You can find mortality schedules online at Ancestry.com or on microfilm at the FHL, FHCs and NARA facilities. Some states' 1850 mortality schedules are searchable for free on FamilySearch.org. And look for published abstracts at genealogical libraries.

▷ **Tips and tricks**
- The 1900 schedule survived only for Minnesota; it's available in *Minnesota 1900 Census Mortality Schedule* by James W. Warren.

VETERANS AND MILITARY CENSUSES

▷ **Revolutionary War pensioners**
YEARS: 1840

WHERE TO FIND IT: *A Census of Pensioners for Revolutionary or Military Services* is available free through Google Books <books.google.com>.

▷ **Civil War veterans schedule**
YEARS: 1890 (half of Kentucky and states following alphabetically)

HOW TO KNOW IF YOUR ANCESTOR IS LISTED: Union veterans and surviving widows for half of Kentucky and the states alphabetically following are listed in this schedule.

WHERE TO FIND IT: The schedules are online at Ancestry.com and on microfilm at the FHL and NARA facilities.

TIPS AND TRICKS: Although enumerators were supposed to count Union veterans, some also recorded those who fought for the South. Officials who reviewed the schedules in Washington, D.C., simply drew lines through the Confederates' names, leaving them still readable.

▷ **Schedules of military personnel on bases and vessels**
YEARS: 1900, 1910, 1920

WHERE TO FIND IT:
• For 1900, these are on NARA microfilm T623, rolls 1,838 to 1,842 (find a Soundex index on film T1081, rolls 1 to 32).

• For 1910, military and naval enumerations are on film T624, roll 1,784; there's no Soundex.

• The 1920 schedules for overseas military and naval forces are on film T625, rolls 2,040 to 2,041; the Soundex is on film M1600, rolls 1 to 18.

▷ **Schedules of merchant seamen on vessels**
YEARS: 1930

WHERE TO FIND IT: Search them on Ancestry.com, or browse them on microfilm at the FHL and NARA.

AMERICAN INDIAN CENSUSES

▷ **Special Indian schedules**
YEARS: 1880, 1900, 1910

HOW TO KNOW IF YOUR ANCESTOR IS LISTED: American Indians who paid taxes were enumerated on the 1880 federal census; those who weren't taxed are listed in Special Census of Indians. For the 1900 and 1910 censuses, American Indians might be listed on special schedules called Inquiries Relating to Indians.

WHERE TO FIND IT: The Special Census of Indians can be found in National Archives micropublication M1791. Inquiries Relating to Indians are with the regular population schedules.

TIPS AND TRICKS: For each household, you may learn the type of dwelling and number of residents, and each person's Indian name, relationship to the head of the household, marital status, tribal status, occupation, education and land ownership status.

▷ **Annual reservation censuses**
YEARS: 1885 to 1940

HOW TO KNOW IF YOUR ANCESTOR IS LISTED: Anyone living on a federal reservation was counted.

WHERE TO FIND IT: Search these censuses on subscription sites Ancestry **<ancestry.com>** and Fold3 **<fold3.com>**. The records also are organized by agency on 692 rolls of microfilm at the FHL and NARA facilities. To determine which rolls you need, download the Indian Census Rolls, 1885–1940 PDF at **<www.archives.gov/research/microfilm/m595.pdf>**.

TIPS AND TRICKS: The Dawes Commission compiled an Indian census card index for schedules from 1898 to 1914 to verify rights to tribal status for the Five Civilized Tribes—Cherokee, Chickasaw, Choctaw, Creek and Seminole. The index is available at the FHL and on NARA's website **<archives.gov>**.

▷ Indian school censuses
YEARS: 1910 to 1939
HOW TO KNOW IF YOUR ANCESTOR IS LISTED: Indian children ages 6 to 18 who attended a reservation school were enumerated.

WHERE TO FIND IT: Look for the schedules in the NARA regional branch covering the area where the tribe was located.

TIPS AND TRICKS: Information collected includes sex, tribe, degree of Indian blood, the distance from home to school, school attendance and a parent's or guardian's name, and often, mother's maiden name.

INTERNATIONAL CENSUSES

9

CANADA

Canada first set out to count its citizens in 1851. That enumeration (some of which has been lost), along with others in 1861 and 1871, covered the four original provinces of Nova Scotia, New Brunswick, Quebec and Ontario (1861 also included Prince Edward Island). After the 1867 establishment of the Dominion of Canada, the national government took over decennial census-taking in 1871. All the Canadian censuses from 1851 to 1911 (the most recent one open to researchers) are online, as are the special 1906 and 1916 censuses of the Prairie Provinces.

YEARS: every 10 years since 1851

WHERE TO FIND IT:
Ancestry.com **<ancestry.com>**

Automated Genealogy **<automatedgenealogy.com>** (indexes to the 1901 and 1911 censuses, as well as a special 1906 census of Alberta, Saskatchewan and Manitoba)

Family History Library **<familysearch.org>** (1881, 1891, 1901 and 1911 are on microfilm; search the 1851, 1871, 1881 and 1891 censuses online.)

Library and Archives of Canada's online Canadian Genealogy Centre **<www.collectionscanada.gc.ca>**

▷ **Tips and tricks**
• For most provinces, censuses in 1851, 1861, 1871, 1881, 1891, 1901, 1906, 1911 and 1916 (this last one was taken only in western provinces) name each person, with age, sex, country or province of birth, religion, racial or ethnic origin, occupation and marital status.

- If you're tracing ancestors in Newfoundland, keep in mind that it didn't join Canada until 1949; you'll find censuses of Newfoundland and Labrador (from 1675 to 1945) at **<ngb.chebucto.org/census.shtml>.**
- The 1666 enumeration of New France, what's now Quebec, is online at **<www.afhs.ab.ca/registry/regqc_census.html>.**

CZECH REPUBLIC
To determine the religion of the population and prospects for conversion, Catholic Habsburg rulers ordered the first Czech census naming people. Parts of this census survive and are on FHL microfilm, and portions of a 1770 census covering Prague are published in a book (search on the keywords *1770 Prague census*).

YEARS: 1651, 1770, 1843, 1857, 1869, 1880, 1890, 1900, 1910, 1921

WHERE TO FIND IT:
District and city archives

Family History Library **<familysearch.org>**

▷ **Tips and tricks**
- Browse images of Czech censuses from 1843 to 1921 at **<familysearch.org>**.
- The FHL also has published copies of Jewish censuses in 1783 (search on the keywords *Jewish families Bohemia 1783*) and 1793 (search on the keywords *1793 Jewish census*).

Although numerous, most Czech enumerations have been lost.

DENMARK

YEARS: 1787, 1801, 1834, 1840, 1845, 1850, 1855, 1860, 1870, 1880, 1885, 1890, 1901, 1906, 1911, 1916, 1921

PRIVACY RESTRICTIONS: records older than 65 years are available to the public

WHERE TO FIND IT:
Danish Demographic Database **<ddd.dda.dk/ddd_en.htm>**

Family History Library **<familysearch.org>** (microfilmed 1845 and 1860 censuses, and portions of various other years)

▷ **Tips and tricks**
- The government will make limited searches in the 1921 and 1925 censuses.
- 1787, 1801, 1834 and 1840 censuses list the names of all members of the household and their ages, sexes, occupations, relationships to the head of the household and marital statuses.
- Censuses from 1845 on list the names, ages, occupations, relationships to the head of the household, religious affiliations and birthplaces (county and parish) of all members of the household.

ENGLAND AND WALES

English censuses have occurred every 10 years since 1801, except for war-torn 1941. The Public Record Office (part of Britain's national archives **<www.nationalarchives.gov.uk>**), which has the originals, historically has kept census records less than 100 years old private.

YEARS: every 10 years since 1801

WHERE TO FIND IT:
Ancestry.com **<ancestry.com>**

Family History Library **<familysearch.org>** (1841–1861 and 1881–1911)

FindMyPast **<www.findmypast.co.uk>**

FreeCEN **<www.freecen.org.uk>** (parts of the 1841–1891)

National Archives 1911 census site **<www.1911census.co.uk>**

Public Record Office **<www.nationalarchives.gov.uk>**

▷ **Tips and tricks**
- The 1841 tally names everyone in a household, listing the person's gender, address, occupation and whether born in England.
- Enumerators typically rounded down ages of anyone over 15 to a multiple of five, so your kin may appear younger than they actually were.
- Censuses from 1851 on list each person's name, age, occupation, relationship to the head of household, and the parish and county of birth.

FINLAND
Finland took a sort of taxation census called *henkikirjat/man-talslängder* beginning in 1634.

YEARS: 1634–1860

WHERE TO FIND IT:
Family History Library **<familysearch.org>**

Finland's National Archives **<digi.narc.fi/digi/?lang=en_us>**

▷ **Tips and tricks**
- From 1634 to 1651, enumerations covered all people older than 12; from 1652 to 1655, those between 15 and 63; from 1655 on, older heads of households were added.
- Nobles and soldiers were exempt until 1765.
- The FHL has filmed Finish census records; they're cataloged by county, with a separate heading for 1810 to 1860 censuses.

FRANCE

Although France first took a national census in 1772, most counts gathered only statistical data. Censuses every five years from 1836 through 1936 did generally collect genealogical data, but these aren't on microfilm. Surviving records (many were destroyed under an 1887 decree) are at departmental archives.

YEARS: every five years from 1836 to 1936, except 1916

WHERE TO FIND IT:
Archives Départementales **<www.francegenweb.org/~archives/archivesgenweb/?id=adfrance>**

▷ **Tips and tricks**
- Some earlier censuses may have been destroyed because of an 1887 decree, but this law was not applied everywhere.
- Enumerations generally list the surname and first names, age, occupation, head of house, nationality and sometimes the birthplace.
- The censuses have not been microfilmed or indexed.

GERMANY

Church records and civil registrations are generally the best records for finding German ancestors, but the FHL does have microfilm of some censuses. Most important are the 1819 census of Mecklenburg-Schwein.

YEARS: 1819 of Mecklenburg-Schwein, 1867, 1890, 1900

WHERE TO FIND IT:
Ancestry.com **<ancestry.com>**

Family History Library **<familysearch.org>** (1819 census on microfilm, online index to 1890 and 1900 censuses)

▷ **Tips and tricks:**
- Censuses for the Danish-held area of Schleswig-Holstein taken in 1769, 1801, 1803, 1834, 1835, 1840, 1845, 1850, 1855 and 1860 can be searched online at the Danish Demographic Database **<ddd.dda.dk/ddd_en.htm>**.
- FamilySearch.org is home to an index of citizen lists for Minden city, 1574–1902.

GREECE

Various rulers of Greece have enumerated the population many times, beginning in the 17th century.

YEARS: 1840 to 1844, 1848, 1851, 1879 from Nauplion; 1835 and 1838–1839 censuses and 1857–1881 and 1889 town registers from Argolidos; and 1923, 1948 and 1953 censuses of the Armenian minority

WHERE TO FIND IT:
Family History Library **<familysearch.org>**

HUNGARY

Although Hungary has a long history of enumerations dating back to 1696, many have been destroyed, and others—kept in county archives under direction of the National Archives of Hungary—are difficult to access. Most useful are those from 1857 and 1869, parts of which are on FHL microfilm.

YEARS: 1857 and 1869 only surviving years

WHERE TO FIND IT:
Family History Library **<familysearch.org>**

▷ **Tips and tricks**
• Jewish researchers will want to check FHL microfilm for several special Jewish censuses taken from 1725 to 1775 and 1848. JewishGen and Ancestry.com offer free searches of that 1848 census, as well as Jewish Names in Property Tax Census, 1828, and Assorted Census Records, 1781–1850.

ITALY

As in most Catholic countries, church records and civil registrations will prove more fruitful than censuses. But the census may help fill in some gaps.

YEARS: every 10 years since 1871

WHERE TO FIND IT:
State archive of each province (Go to Italy GenWeb **<www. italywgw.org/region>** and click a region, then a province.)

▷ **Tips and tricks**
- Enumerations from 1871 to 1901 are not uniform in content, and in most regions, only name the head of household, his occupation and the number of persons in the household.
- Enumerations from 1911 on list the names, ages, occupations, relationships to the head of the household and birthplaces of each member of a household.

IRELAND

Although the Irish government first took a census in 1813 and continued every 10 years from 1821 to 1911, most of those early enumerations have been lost to fire or to bureaucrats who destroyed them after compiling statistics. The 1901 and 1911 censuses are the only complete counts open to the public.

YEARS: about every 10 years since 1813

WHERE TO FIND IT:
Family History Library **<familysearch.org>** (microfilm of early fragments, complete 1901 and 1911 censuses)

National Archives of Ireland
<www.census.nationalarchives.ie>

▷ **Tips and tricks**
- The 1901 and 1911 censuses list every household member, with age, sex, relationship, religion, occupation, marital status, county of birth (country only for foreign births), literacy and whether the person spoke Irish.
- The 1911 count also asked each married women the length of time she'd been married to her current husband, number of children and number of living children.
- Look for Irish ancestors in various church tallies and taxation records, such as Griffith's Valuation (1847 to 1864).
- Records of some 60,000 heads of household in the 1851

Dublin City Census survived a 1922 Public Record Office fire and are on the subscription Irish Origins site **<www.irishorigins.com>**.

MEXICO

Pre-independence Mexican censuses include a 1689 enumeration of Spaniards in Mexico City, published in a book, *Gente de España en la Ciudad de México, Año de 1689* (available from the FHL), and territorial censuses that the *Real Ordenanza* (royal decree) of 1786 ordered every five years. The FHL has 110 volumes of these and some earlier censuses, plus an index, on a microfilm series called *Padrones*, 1752–1865. Each census covered a specific group, such as men in the military or in commerce, but enumerating every five years proved an elusive goal.

Post-independence, the Mexican government tried to take censuses in 1868 and 1878, but didn't gain wide cooperation from the populace until 1895. Decennial censuses began in 1900.

YEARS: 1868, 1878, 1895, 1900–1930

WHERE TO FIND IT:
Family History Library **<familysearch.org>**

Mexico's National Archives **<www.agn.gob.mx>**

▷ **Tips and tricks**
- Many original returns have been destroyed. A few are on FHL microfilm, cataloged by locality.
- The 1930 Mexican census is available on the FamilySearch website.

NETHERLANDS

Dutch national censuses began in 1829 and continued every 10 years until 1929, followed by tallies in 1947, 1960 and 1971. The records are kept locally, in municipal archives (stadsarchief), and only some are on FHL microfilm (run a place search on the town name).

YEARS: every 10 years from 1829 to 1929; 1947, 1960 and 1971

WHERE TO FIND IT:
Municipal archives

Family History Library **<familysearch.org>**

▷ **Tips and tricks**
- A few local censuses also are on FHL film for the provinces of Friesland (1689, 1714, 1744, 1796) and Overijssel (1748, 1795).
- Browse images of the Noord-Brabant Province Population Registers 1820–1930 at <familysearch.org>.

NORWAY

Among the earliest Norwegian censuses were the civil and clerical counts taken from 1664 to 1666. These censuses covered only rural areas, and some parts have been lost. The first true nationwide nominative census was taken in 1801.

YEARS: between 1664 and 1666, 1701, 1801, 1865, 1875, 1891, 1900, 1910

WHERE TO FIND IT:
Family History Library **<familysearch.org>**

Norwegian national archives free Digitalarkivet site <**arkivverket.no/Digitalarkivet**>

▷ **Tips and tricks:**
- Census between 1664 and 1666 included heads of household, plus males over age 12
- The 1701 census is incomplete and enumerated all males age 1 and older living in rural areas.
- The 1801 census listed all family members, relationships, ages and occupations.
- The 1865, 1875, 1891, 1900 and 1910 censuses include birthplace, farm data and religion, if other than the state Lutheran church.
- The Digitalarkivet also includes a number of enumerations for military and tax purposes.

ROMANIA
YEARS: Austro-Hungarian Empire censuses of Transylvania, Banat and Bukovina in 1785, 1805, 1828, 1857, 1869, 1880, 1890, 1900 and 1910; Romanian censuses in 1912, 1930, 1941, 1956 and 1966

WHERE TO FIND IT:
National Archives of Romania <**www.arhivelenationale. ro/?lan=1**>

National Archives of Hungary <**www.mol.gov.hu/?akt_ menu=574&set_lang=466**>

Family History Library <**familysearch.org**> (Austro-Hungarian census records, covering parts of Transylvania)

▷ **Tips and tricks**
- A 1942 Jewish census, also covering Moldova and Ukraine, is available on JewishGen and Ancestry.com.

RUSSIA

The only complete population census conducted in Imperial Russia was 1897. The FHL has microfilmed the 1897 records for some areas; run a place search of the FHL catalog for *Russia* and look under the Census heading for details.

YEARS: 1897

WHERE TO FIND IT:
Family History Library <**familysearch.org**>

Ancestry.com <**ancestry.com**>

JewishGen <**jewishgen.org**>

▷ **Tips and tricks**
- Ancestry.com and JewishGen have free indexes to portions of several Russian censuses and census substitutes, including Duma Voter Lists, 1906–1907; Jewish Families in Russian Empire Census, 1897; Grodno Gubernia Voters List, 1912; and Jewish Religious Personnel, 1853–1854.
- Questions included family name, given name, patronymic or nickname, gender, relation to the head of the family or household, age, marital status, social status, birthplace, residence, faith, language spoken, literacy and occupation.

SCOTLAND

Scottish censuses largely match those for England and Wales, with genealogically valuable enumerations available for every decade from 1841 through 1911.

YEARS: every 10 years since 1841

WHERE TO FIND IT:
Ancestry.com <**ancestry.com**>

Ancestry.co.uk **<ancestry.co.uk>**

Family History Library **<familysearch.org>** (microfilm of 1841–1891, complete 1881 surname index)

ScotlandsPeople **<www.scotlandspeople.gov.uk>**

▷ **Tips and tricks**
- The 1841 tally names everyone in a household, listing the person's gender, address, occupation and whether born in England.
- Enumerators typically rounded down ages of anyone over 15 to a multiple of five, so your kin may appear younger than they actually were.
- Censuses from 1851 on list each person's name, age, occupation, relationship to the head of household, and the parish and county of birth.

SPAIN
Church records are much more important than censuses for finding Spanish ancestors.

YEARS: 1591, 1749–1956

WHERE TO FIND IT:
Family History Library **<familysearch.org>**

▷ **Tips and tricks**
- The Ministerio de Cultura has published the section called *Respuestas Generales of the Marques de Catastro de Ensenada* (1749–1956) online at **<pares.mcu.es>**.

SWEDEN

Although church records—including registers that amount to annual parish censuses—are the most important tool for tracing Swedes, censuses can be a useful supplement.

YEARS: sporadic partial enumerations 1620–1860; 1880, 1900

WHERE TO FIND IT:
Family History Library **<familysearch.org>** (1620–1860 on microfilm)

SVAR **<www.svar.ra.se>** (1880, 1890 and 1900 censuses, plus a few 1860 and 1870 counties)

▷ **Tips and tricks:**
• Beginning in 1652, censuses listed those between ages 15 and 63; after 1841, between 17 and 63; after 1887, 18 to 63. Soldiers, who were exempt from taxes, were omitted, but their families were listed. Nobles and their families, also exempt, were generally skipped until 1810.
• The 1890 census for Norrbotten, Västerbotten, Västernorrland, Jämtland and Värmland is free online at **<www.foark.umu.se/census>**.

GOOGLE TRANSLATE

As you research international censuses you will likely encounter non-English language websites. When this happens, use Google Translate **<translate.google.com>** to translate the sites' contents and continue your research.

▷ **To translate an entire website**
1. Type or copy and paste the web address in the search box on the Google Translate home page **<translate.google.com>** and hit Enter. Google will pull up the website so it appears within the Google Translate Page.

2. Identify the language of the website and then select that language in the From pull-down menu in the Google Translate box at the top of the page. In the To pull-down menu select English. Click Translate.

3. The page will reappear with an English language translation.

4. Flip back and forth between the original-language version of the website and the English translation by clicking either the Translation or Original View option in the Google Translate heading.

▷ **To translate a passage of text to English**
1. Copy and paste the text you want to translate into the search box on the Google Translate home page **<translate. google.com>**.

2. Identify the language the text is written in and select that language in the From pull-down menu.

3. Select English in the To pull-down menu.

4. Click Translate.

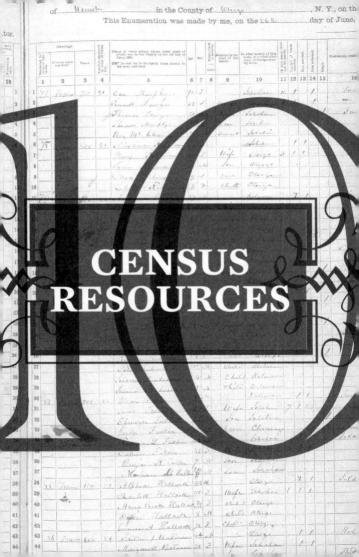

CENSUS RESOURCES

Have more questions about census schedules? These reliable sources should answer them.

BOOKS

The American Census: A Social History by Margo J. Anderson (Yale University Press)

The American Census Handbook by Thomas Jay Kemp (Scholarly Resources)

The Census Book: A Genealogist's Guide to Federal Census Facts, Schedules and Indexes by William Dollarhide (Heritage Quest)

A Census of Pensioners for Revolutionary or Military Services, 1840 by the US Department of State (Genealogical Publishing Co.)

The Census Tables for the French Colony of Louisiana From 1699 Through 1732 by Charles R. Maduell Jr. (Genealogical Publishing Co.)

A Century of Population Growth from the First Census of the United States to the Twelfth, 1790–1900 by the Bureau of the Census (Genealogical Publishing Co.)

The Family Tree Resource Book for Genealogists edited by Sharon DeBartolo Carmack and Erin Nevius (Family Tree Books)

Finding Answers in US Census Records by Loretto Dennis Szucs and Matthew Wright (Ancestry)

Guide to Genealogical Research in the National Archives of the United States, 3rd edition, edited by Anne Bruner Eales and Robert S. Kvasnicka (NARA)

Heads of Families at the First Census of the United States Taken in the Year 1790, 12 volumes (Clearfield Co.)

Map Guide to the U.S. Federal Censuses, 1790–1920 by William Thorndale and William Dollarhide (Genealogical Publishing Co.)

Measuring America: The Decennial Censuses From 1790 to 2000 (US Government Printing Office)

State Census Records by Ann S. Lainhart (Genealogical Publishing Co.)

Your Guide to the Federal Census by Kathleen W. Hinckley (Betterway Books)

WEBSITES: RESEARCH HELPS AND PORTALS

1930 CENSUS
<1930census.archives.gov>
NARA's "comprehensive guide" gives search strategies and answers to frequently asked questions about the 1930 census.

1940 CENSUS
<www.archives.gov/research/census/1940>
Browse FAQs about the 1940 census, read up on social history and view a map of the United States from the time period.

AFRIGENEAS
<www.afrigeneas.com/aacensus>
View African-American census schedules and records by state.

ALL CENSUS
<www.allcensus.com>
Request lookups for the 1881 Canadian census or click on a US state and peruse county listings.

ANCESTRY.COM
<www.ancestry.com>
Search images of all available US censuses with a US subscription. The site offers every-name indexes covering 1790 to 1940, and has indexes to many special schedules.

ARCHIVES.COM
<www.archives.com>
Search more than 500 million records on this subscription site.

BEGINNER'S GUIDE TO THE US FEDERAL CENSUSES
<www.tngenweb.org/census>
Check this site for basic information about census takers, places to find censuses and more.

CENSUS FACTS
<www.heritagequest.com/censusfacts>
Find out what information each federal census collected, the states and territories covered and other census specifics.

CENSUS FINDER
<www.censusfinder.com>
Pick a state from the pull-down menu for links to online record sources.

CENSUS LINKS
<www.censuslinks.com>
Click the United States link, then select a state and county to surf related census material.

CENSUS ONLINE
<www.census-online.com>
You'll find links to enumerations on both free and subscription websites.

CENSUS RECORDS: INTRODUCTION AND LINKS TO RESOURCES
<www.archives.gov/research/census>
Access NARA's online guide to getting and using federal census records.

CYNDI'S LIST: US CENSUS
<www.cyndislist.com/census.htm>
Link to census help sites and records sources, organized by year.

ENUMERATION FORMS
<usa.ipums.org/usa/voliii/tEnumForm.shtml>
Find the forms and instructions given to census takers for the 1860 to 2000 federal censuses.

FAMILY TREE MAGAZINE FORMS
<familytreemagazine.com/freeforms>
Download free extraction worksheets for every federal census.

FAMILYSEARCH: CENSUS RECORDS
<familysearch.org>
Church of Jesus Christ of Latter-day Saints volunteers have transcribed all or portions of the US censuses from 1850 to 1930. Many collections contain original images, and they are searchable online for free.

FAMILYSEARCH: RESEARCH HELPS
<familysearch.org/eng/search/rg/frameset_rhelps.asp>
Select Sorted by Subject to get to an alphabetical subject index where you can locate links to census research guides for each state.

GENEALOGY.COM US CENSUS COLLECTION
<www.genealogy.com>

View images of all extant federal census records; head-of-household indexes cover 1790 to 1820, 1860, 1870 and 1900 to 1920. The images and indexes in this subscription collection are identical to those on HeritageQuest Online (below)—the result of a licensing arrangement between the two companies.

HERITAGEQUEST ONLINE
<www.heritagequestonline.com>

Only institutions can subscribe to this complete collection of federal census images, with most years indexed by head of household. But if your library or genealogical society has a subscription, you can tap into that data for free—maybe even from home (ask your librarian about remote access). To access unindexed 1830 to 1850, 1880 and 1930 images, click Browse in the upper-left corner.

HISTORICAL CENSUS BROWSER
<mapserver.lib.virginia.edu>

You won't find data on your ancestors, but the information presented here describes the population and economy of US states and counties from 1790 to 1960.

MORTALITYSCHEDULES.COM
<mortalityschedules.com>

Search an index of records of people who died within the 12 month preceding the censuses taken in 1850 to 1880.

NARA: NONPOPULATION CENSUS RECORDS
<www.archives.gov/research/census/nonpopulation>

View all NARA has to offer by way of nonpopulation records, including agriculture, mortality and social statistics schedules for the census years of 1850, 1860, 1870 and 1880, as well as manufacturing schedules for 1820, 1850, 1860, 1870 and 1880.

OBTAINING ENUMERATION DISTRICTS FOR THE CENSUS IN ONE STEP
<stevemorse.org/census>
If you know your city-dwelling ancestor's town and street, use this site to identify enumeration districts for the 1910 to 1930 censuses.

ORPHANS' HOME
<freepages.genealogy.rootsweb.ancestry.com/ ~orphanshome>
View state-by-state transcriptions of orphans, adoptees and foster children recorded in the US and Canadian censuses.

SEARCHING THE US CENSUS BY NAME IN ONE STEP
<stevemorse.org/census/ancestry.html>
Ancestry.com subscribers get more flexible census searching here.

US CENSUS BUREAU: SOCIAL STATISTICS
<www.census.gov/prod/www/abs/decennial>
Results and statistics from every enumeration can be found here.

USGENWEB ARCHIVES
<usgwarchives.net/census>
Find census-page images (you also can volunteer to index the images) for most states, though some states have only a handful of counties and years.

USGENWEB CENSUS PROJECT
<www.us-census.org>
USGenNet, a splinter group from the original USGenWeb, offers a search form and a chart of available transcriptions and scanned images.

WEBSITES: STATE INDEXES AND IMAGES

1849 MINNESOTA TERRITORIAL CENSUS
<www.parkbooks.com/Html/res_18-1.html>
Look for your Minnesota ancestors in this online copy of the state's first territorial census, reprinted from the Minnesota Genealogical Journal.

1880 CENSUS RECORDS OF MONTANA
<freepages.genealogy.rootsweb.ancestry.com/~xander/montana-census.htm>
Download a free list of 22,666 residents (of the 39,159 total) enumerated in the 1880 Montana Territory census.

AGRICULTURAL AND MANUFACTURING CENSUS RECORDS OF 15 SOUTHERN STATES FOR THE YEARS 1850, 1860, 1870 AND 1880
<www.archive.org/details/unc_chapel_hill_agricultural_manufacturing_census_records_1880>
Download a copy of these enumerations for North Carolina, Kentucky, Tennessee, Georgia, Louisiana, Florida, Maryland, Mississippi, West Virginia, Alabama, Virginia and Texas.

COLORADO STATE ARCHIVES: 1870 CENSUS INDEX
<www.colorado.gov/dpa/doit/archives/1870>
Click on an alphabetical surname range and look for your ancestor in this browsable index.

DAKOTA TERRITORY 1860 CENSUS
<www.rootsweb.ancestry.com/cgi-bin/sdcensus/sd1860cen.pl>
Search this pre-statehood enumeration by surname.

DAKOTA TERRITORY 1885 CENSUS
<library.ndsu.edu/archives/databases/1885-census>
This database covers all of present-day North Dakota. Search by name, birthplace or residence.

HISTORIC PITTSBURGH CENSUS SCHEDULES
<digital.library.pitt.edu/census/census_name.html>
Search federal census data for Pittsburgh from 1850 to 1880, and Allegheny City from 1850 through 1870.

IDAHO STATE HISTORICAL SOCIETY: 1890 IDAHO CENSUS
<history.idaho.gov/idaho-1890-reconstructed-census>
View a copy of the 1890 census index, recently reconstructed by volunteers, covering select Idaho counties.

KANSAS CENSUS—FEDERAL AND STATE, 1855 TO 1930
<www.kshs.org/p/kansas-censuses-1855-1930/10961>
The Kansas State Historical Society offers a smattering of online indexes to state and federal censuses. Click on the link for each census year to find out what's available.

LIBRARY OF MICHIGAN 1870 CENSUS INDEX
<mdoe.state.mi.us/1870census>
You can search this index by name, county or township.

MARYLAND STATE ARCHIVES CENSUS INDEXES
<www.mdarchives.state.md.us/msa/refserv/html/censussearch.html>
Search indexes of the 1776 and 1778 state censuses, the 1870 federal census for 22 counties plus Baltimore, and the 1880 federal census for Anne Arundel County.

NEVADA'S ONLINE CENSUS DATABASE
<nvshpo.org/index.php?option=com_content&view=article&id=1278&Itemid=391>
The Silver State is the first to put all its federal census data online—1860, 1870, 1880, 1900, 1910 and 1920.

NEW YORK STATE CENSUS
<www.frontiernet.net/~halsey1/ny/ny-census.htm>
This informative site provides microfilm numbers for New York

state censuses. It also links to data for the 1720 Albany, 1714 Dutchess, 1702 Orange and 1689 Ulster county censuses.

OREGON STATE ARCHIVES: CENSUS RECORDS
<arcweb.sos.state.or.us/censuslist.html>
Access indexes to state censuses for the years 1865, 1875, 1885 and 1895.

SPECIAL MAINE 1837 CENSUS
<www.rootsweb.ancestry.com/~meandrhs/history/us debt/census/maine/1837.html>
To view data from this enumeration, select a locality. Find links to special censuses for Wisconsin, Iowa, Kansas, Minnesota, Oregon, Florida and the Dakotas at the bottom of the page.

UTAH CENSUS SEARCH
<www.xmission.com/~nelsonb/census_search.htm>
Look for Utah Territory ancestors from 1850 to 1880.

WASHINGTON HISTORICAL RECORDS SEARCH
<www.secstate.wa.gov/history/search.aspx>
Scour territorial census records from 1847 to 1892, plus the entire 1910 census of Washington. A searchable index is online at <www.digitalarchives.wa.gov>.

CANADIAN AND UK RECORDS

1901 CENSUS FOR ENGLAND AND WALES
<www.1901censusonline.com>
Search this census index for free, then pay to see transcribed details on a person and view a record image.

ANCESTRY.COM UK AND IRELAND COLLECTION
<ancestry.com>
A subscription gets you linked images and indexes for the

1871, 1891 and 1901 censuses of England, Wales, the Channel Islands and the Isle of Man.

AUTOMATED GENEALOGY
<automatedgenealogy.com>
So far, the indexes to the 1901, 1906 and 1911 Canadian censuses have been transcribed. Search on a name, then use the geographic data to find a record image at the National Archives of Canada website **<www.collectionscanada.gc.ca>**, which you can search by location only.

BRITISH ORIGINS: ENGLAND AND WALES CENSUS 1841
<www.britishorigins.com>
For a yearly fee, you can search the earliest enumeration to list everyone living at a residence, rather than just the head of household.

FAMILYSEARCH: CENSUS RECORDS
<www.familysearch.org>
Search indexes of the England and Wales censuses for 1841–1861 and 1881–1911, and Canadian censuses 1851, 1871, 1881 and 1891 for free.

FREECEN: UK CENSUS ONLINE
<freecen.rootsweb.com>
This database results from a volunteer project to transcribe the 1841 through 1871 and 1891 UK censuses. Click on Database Coverage to see progress on your ancestral county.

THE GENEALOGIST
<www.thegenealogist.co.uk>
The Census Name-Indexing Project has transcribed 1841 to 1911 UK census information and made it available online. To view an index for a county during a particular census year, you need to purchase a subscription.

ORGANIZATIONS

FAMILY HISTORY LIBRARY
35 N. West Temple St.
Salt Lake City, UT 84150
(800) 346-6044
<www.familysearch.org>

NATIONAL ARCHIVES AND RECORDS ADMINISTRATION
700 Pennsylvania Ave. NW
Washington, DC 20408
(866) 272-6272
<www.archives.gov>

UK NATIONAL ARCHIVES
Kew, Richmond, Surrey
TW9 4DU, England

RESEARCH
TRACKER

Use this chart to track census records you have
researched for each ancestor.

Census Records for

_____

(Ancestor's Name)

RESEARCH TRACKER

1790	
1800	
1810	
1820	
1830	
1840	
1850	
1860	
1870	
1880	
1890	
1900	
1910	
1920	
1930	
1940	

Census Records for

_____

(Ancestor's Name)

1790	
1800	
1810	
1820	
1830	
1840	
1850	
1860	
1870	
1880	
1890	
1900	
1910	
1920	
1930	
1940	

Census Records for

_____

(Ancestor's Name)

1790	
1800	
1810	
1820	
1830	
1840	
1850	
1860	
1870	
1880	
1890	
1900	
1910	
1920	
1930	
1940	

RESEARCH TRACKER

Census Records for

_____

(Ancestor's Name)

1790	
1800	
1810	
1820	
1830	
1840	
1850	
1860	
1870	
1880	
1890	
1900	
1910	
1920	
1930	
1940	

Census Records for

_____

(Ancestor's Name)

1790	
1800	
1810	
1820	
1830	
1840	
1850	
1860	
1870	
1880	
1890	
1900	
1910	
1920	
1930	
1940	

RESEARCH TRACKER

Census Records for

_____

(Ancestor's Name)

1790	
1800	
1810	
1820	
1830	
1840	
1850	
1860	
1870	
1880	
1890	
1900	
1910	
1920	
1930	
1940	

Census Records for

_____

(Ancestor's Name)

1790	
1800	
1810	
1820	
1830	
1840	
1850	
1860	
1870	
1880	
1890	
1900	
1910	
1920	
1930	
1940	

RESEARCH TRACKER

Census Records for

_____

(Ancestor's Name)

1790	
1800	
1810	
1820	
1830	
1840	
1850	
1860	
1870	
1880	
1890	
1900	
1910	
1920	
1930	
1940	

....

....

....

....

....

....

....

....

....

....

....

....

....

....

....

....

....

....

....

....

....

....

....

....

....

Acknowledgments

The content in this book was adapted from contributions by these *Family Tree Magazine* writers and genealogy experts.

Sharon DeBartolo Carmack

Allison Dolan

David A. Fryxell

Diane Haddad

Kathleen W. Hinkley

Jamie Royce